THE INDEPENDENT SALES REP

How To Be Successful
As An Independent Sales Rep,
and How To Use An Independent Sales Rep
Successfully In Any Business

WILLIAM CORNELL

ISBN: 1-4392-2415-3
ISBN-13: 9781439224151

Visit www.booksurge.com to order additional copies.

TABLE OF CONTENTS

ACKNOWLEDGEMENTS 7

INTRODUCTION. 9
- Who Can Use This Book
- Why The Need For This Book
- How Is This Book Different From Others

CHAPTER 1 13
Independent Sales Reps- What Are They & Why Needed
- Why Companies Use Them
- Why Sales Professionals Become Independents

CHAPTER 2 23
The Independent Rep Process & How It Should Work
- Communications
- Support From Company
- Samples
- Catalogs & Other Marketing Material

CHAPTER 3 41
What It Takes To Be An Independent Sales Rep
- Entrepreneurial Attitude
- Organizational Skills
- Persistence
- Flexibility—Ability to Change & Vary

CHAPTER 4 50
Supplies & Setup Needed
- Location-Showroom/Office vs. Home Office
- Solo Or With A Team; Subreps
- Support Staff? or Not
- Supplies, Equipment—Car, Office Items
  (computer, fax, phone, cell, copier, etc).
- Budget Concerns—mail, phone bills, travel, rent
- Outside support—Legal, Taxes, etc.

CHAPTER 5 . . . .**68**
Matching Rep to Company
- Trade Shows
- Published Rep Guides and Directories
- Websites
- Referrals
- Your Résumé
- A Word To Vendors Seeking Sales Reps

CHAPTER 6 . . . .**85**
Troubleshooting and Problem Solving
- Troubleshooting To Get The Sale
- Troubleshooting Faulty Vendors
- Troubleshooting Dishonest Vendors
- Personality Clashes With Vendors
- Troubleshooting Problems With Customer Relations
- Troubleshooting Commissions Owed You

CHAPTER 7 . . . .**107**
The Sales Process Itself
- Match the line to the account— where your contacts come in handy
- Leads—acting on them and follow-up
- Regular Customer Contact—personal
- Contact Via email, mail, phone, etc. (The Hopper System)

CHAPTER 8 . . . .**135**
Small Accounts
- They add up!
- Money is immediate/commission rate better
- Feedback/Friendship potential is good
- The Gentleman and Chorus Girl

CHAPTER 9 . . . . **144**
Large Accounts
- Compliance-more important than how good your product is.
- EDI, UPCs, Ethics, Performance Standards
- What to Look for in Compliance Manuals and Chargeback Schedules
- Payoff Greater, Reorders Automatic
- The Pitch and the P.O.

CHAPTER 10 . . . . **162**
Changing World—Sales of the Future
- Technology and Trends—Keep Up With Them
- Marketing vs. Simple Sales
- Keep educating yourself—Increase Your Value—Caddy vs. "Bag-toter"
- What's more important—your portfolio of companies or your account base?
- Keep Making It Fun, Interesting

BIBLIOGRAPHY/WEB RESOURCES **179**

GLOSSARY **185**

AUTHOR BIOGRAPHY **191**

INDEX **193**

ACKNOWLEDGEMENTS

There have been plenty of family, friends, and business acquaintances whom I've learned from and been inspired by over the decades. Some I've lost touch with, others are still going strong.

In spite of griping at me to cut my hair, do the chores, etc., while I was growing up, my late Dad, Barry Cornell, turned out to be a big supporter in almost anything I did, be it my work, my amateurish musical experiments, or my writing. He didn't get to see this finished product, but I hope he would have enjoyed it. My Mom Sally is a great sounding board on everything I do, say, or think, so I hope she can find something in this book of interest and let me know how to improve it.

I've learned a lot from my work and experiences with the Marmadukes: John, Steve, and their late great father Sam, plus Gene Tornatore, Michael Bayler, Bruce Goldberg, Brandon Batton, and Pug Pagliara, whose tales of the early, post WWII record business are still instructive to me. Too bad the music industry has few such minds today.

Customers who've stuck with me through two marriages, three or four cars, two mortgages, perhaps hundreds of lines: K.C. Hamill, Shelly Meyer, Jeff Hammer, Lisa Puff, Stan Stack, Clarisa Pena, Eric Atchely, Wes Nichols, the Qureshi Bros & Ali, Akbar Udawala, Alicia Shultz, the Eckstroms, Sam Peil, Bill Wisener, Rich Trudeau, Hayes & John at

Waterloo, Nancy Barnard, the Fagerquists, the Haglers, Rachel Wilson, Shane Lopez, Tom Houston, Thais Willis, Connie Bible, Quinn Bishop, Tom Logan, Tom Shomaker, Mick Clark, Ben Lincoln, Bucks Burnett. There are plenty more, and I haven't forgotten them; these are the ones that go back the longest and are still around.

In an industry that has the longevity of, say, the average housefly, it's great to still have people to work for and with like Mike Taylor, Dell Furano, Linda Judy, Wes Bockley, Patrick Smith, Allen Dench, Jim George, Mary Sansone, Andrea and Mike Howard as well as fellow reps like Lance Stokes, Mark Kessell, Rick Fox, Rocky Wattigney and Reade White-Spunner.

Special Thanks to David Soriano who came along at the perfect time and has helped me sell for more than a decade with little more than me telling him, "Here, have at it." When describing the qualities of the perfect associate to team up with, he's got them.

INTRODUCTION

A. Why The Need For This Book

After being a casual fan of the business book for years, observing one school of thought after another, I realized one day that there aren't that many books that told the world about what it was I did for a living.

And I really love doing what I do for a living—surely this can't be kept all to us who are independent, multi-line sales representatives!

The few books out there are good, and I can tell they are written by kindred souls...but make no bones about it. What we do may be enjoyable, but it is not easy, and it is not for everyone. These other books did not deal with certain aspects of our work that I felt important.

B. How Is This Book Different From Others

Most other books out there dealing with this subject are simply sales-oriented; they could be used by an inside salesman or an indie rep, but they're not specific enough for the latter. If we were talking football, these books would simply focus in on how to play quarterback. Nothing would be said about blocking, receiving passes, running backs...or defense...or building a team through drafts, trades, free agents, etc. In other words, they left out some important stuff.

So I set out to write a book that covered some of those things, but I also included subjects such as:

- If being a salesperson means selling solutions in today's world, how to trouble-shoot and look for solutions to existing problems and possible future problems.
- How to find new vendors. This subject gets glossed over in most of the books I've seen, yet it is just as important to sell yourself to a potential new vendor you'll sell for, as it is to sell a vendor's goods. We'll go into detail about this later.
- Looking at Sales Reps in reverse—that is, what if you are a vendor? What to look for in an indie rep, what to expect from him, what he should expect from you. There were a few books out there that touched on this subject but they were priced so only a Fortune 500 company could afford them. Many companies that can benefit from an indie rep relationship are small startups. A sales force that costs them nothing in salaries, benefits, training expenses, etc., is often a very logical solution. Why stick these fledgling companies with a book that costs them a weeks' worth of groceries?
- Marketing is just as important, if not more so, than sales in today's world. Other books touch on marketing but may not go into as much detail as we hope to in this book. For one thing, they may not clarify the question, "Just what is marketing anyway?" There are a million ways to define marketing in today's world, and most of them are nowhere near correct.
- And there are more subjects we hope to discuss that haven't been put under one cover before...

C. Who Can Use This Book?

Companies are outsourcing more new functions every day. Big or small, you see Accounting, Human Resources, Information Technology (IT) and many more functions sourced to outside companies. Why not sales? It's already happening in many industries, not just my own.

Ever buy insurance? Many ads for insurance give you contact information for the company, but many times, once you call them, they may refer you to an "independent agent." One of the more famous insurance agents in the Dallas - Ft Worth area had access to hundreds of insurance policies. In my own experience, I purchased a health plan that would lock in premium rates for thirty-six months, a very attractive alternative. However, I asked him, "What if they sock it to me after the end of thirty-six months?" He replied, "Then call me; I have access to other plans and we'll start you in on another that has competitive premium rates."

That's just one of the beauties of an independent sales rep—which is exactly what an independent insurance agent is. And by the way, when you're self-employed as an independent sales rep, you will need to provide your own health insurance, so become familiar with your independent insurance agents in your area—chances are very good they will be your source for a plan that's geared to your needs.

If you've spent a few years in a business and have developed an entrepreneurial bent (there are other books out there that will cover that subject in more detail), the option to be an independent, multi-line sales representative may be perfect for you. I honestly don't know every industry out there that uses indie reps—licensed goods, fashion, elements of the music and entertainment business are just the ones I am experienced in. We've seen that insurance does too.

Even if an industry is satisfied with relying upon inside sales staffs, outsourcing even a portion of their sales and marketing efforts would have to present itself as a pretty attractive proposal...especially when it means it will cost the company a lot less for its efforts.

So I'd say this book is good for anyone, in any industry who'd like to strike out on his or her own in a low-overhead career. You could be a victim of a layoff, or firing...or just wanted something new in a vocation using the knowledge you have of your chosen industry. It will also help those who are on the production side of things who want to understand who an independent rep is and what to expect from such a relationship.

I won't be so cocky as to say this is the only book you'll ever need...but it could be the first book to use, and I hope the best overall.

CHAPTER 1

Independent Sales Reps—
What Are They, And Why Are They Needed?

Let's start out by agreeing that the world needs sales-men/saleswomen. It's been that way throughout history—and may indeed be one of the world's oldest honorable professions.

Many empires expanded not just by military means, but by traders who bought new and exciting goods from afar to bring back to sell to their homeland. The Prophet Muhammad was a salesman. Venetian explorer/trader Marco Polo and his family were salesmen. Most of the entire Age of Discovery was fueled by sales professionals who knew where to get spices to enliven the rather bland food of Renaissance Europe, or where to find precious metals to turn into currency to buy more stuff.

Cities like Venice (a swamp), Mecca (a small oasis in a brutal desert), Hong Kong (a bunch of big rocks on the water—somewhat how the British Colonial authority first described it), Singapore (another swamp) were built by salesmen who turned them into dynamic trade centers. Who else in their right mind would have lived in any of those places to begin with? A big world got smaller—and better—as a result of salesmen/saleswomen and sales centers such as these.

The point is this: Middlemen—like today's independent sales reps—are valuable since they not only know the right customer—and prospect-contacts. Good mid-dlemen (and –women) usually know how to sell stuff better than the guys who produce the goods in the first place...and it's been that way for centuries. It'll probably continue into the future.

The likelihood of technology completely eliminating the salesman or -woman is scant. Twenty years ago, auto-mated radio stations and phone reception systems were all the rage; yet people still prefer to listen to a real radio host and talk to a live person—and these points are of-ten brought up in marketing messages for such compa-nies as being a distinct advantage over their competitors, who are still playing a boring radio format with canned announcers, or a customer service on-hold message that asks you to punch so many buttons you forget what you called for to begin with.

A. Why Companies Use Independent Sales Reps

Of course, many companies hire their own sales force that they have control over. But many companies look to outside professionals, Independent (or, Indie) Multi-Line Sales Reps to either supplement their inside sales staff or to completely handle their sales efforts.

Reasons why include:
- Economics: Indie Reps are usually commission-only. They require little or no costly benefits packages, training, or real estate to house them while they work in the office. They get paid only what they are worth. But...that commission usually makes the effort on the sales rep's part worthwhile!
- An Existing Account Base: Indie Reps already have an account base and established relationships that they've earned the trust of. Particularly for new com-panies, this saves them a lot of effort in trying to get their own reputation established. When a customer

says, "Well, if Joe says they're good, they must be," the company can add a customer to their list that may have taken much longer with which to establish a relationship. Since good reps often carry several or many lines within an industry, this will also be an advantage to a company wanting to get noticed— even if it risks being overshadowed by competitors the rep also sells.

- Product or Industry Expertise: Since they have experience with several or many lines within an industry, good sales reps can sell solutions, not just the product. A company can, and ought to, listen to their opinions on how to best make the product in question sell to the prospective accounts. Problems occur when many companies have not researched their product to begin with and expect the salesman/saleswoman to work miracles. Having sales reps act as mediators between vendor and customer becomes a plus for both sides particularly when those two sides may not speak the same lingo or understand each other's positions. Sales reps can also present solutions to the customer, particularly if that customer is new to the product in question. "How do we display this stuff? Which styles or flavors work best?" If you were a buyer, who'd you rather listen to, an independent rep that's more apt to be objective and wants your business for the long run, or a company rep who'll tell you everything he or she sells is great?

I think the future looks positive for independent sales reps since so many companies continue to outsource so many functions. And I don't think this is something some call center in India, Singapore, or Timbuktu can handle for accounts here in the USA (or Canada). I think they will need sales professionals based right here to do that job.

Let's discuss companies that are on the other end of the spectrum—those looking to buy. Why should an account or customer want to deal with an Indie Sales Rep?

- Established relationship and trust for existing products and any new ones the rep picks up.
- Unbiased opinion...the reps will not lie to an account if they know what's good for them. After all, they have other lines to potentially sell the account. The good reps will often emphasize the products that will best suit that account.
- Far-reaching knowledge of the marketplace, since the rep is familiar with multiple lines and products, as well as accounts.
- But...if they're good they won't overload themselves to the point where they have so many lines they often forget to mention what may be important news to an account. Think of the salesperson equivalent to an overbooked attorney—a good rep will not allow this to happen.
- The Indie rep will keep the account in the loop because he or she has to! Sales reps are paid commissions-only, remember. If they don't get orders they starve. An inside sales staffer may be content with the base salary he/she gets and commission for that fat account over in the next town. A good indie rep is an entrepreneur and, by definition, does not have a dependent mentality...the independent rep has an independent mentality that entrepreneurs must have. We'll deal with this later...

B. Why Sales Professionals Become Independent Reps

Now, let's say you're an inside salesman, or any other professional who has an entrepreneurial itch. Why should you consider becoming an independent sales rep?

- Money: you'll likely make more of it as an indie as opposed to being an inside sales rep. Because you can add or drop lines at will, you can focus on the possibilities that will earn you most reward.

- Freedom: again, you have more control over what you sell. You may enter into agreements that prevent you from selling lines that directly compete with each other, as some industries are less flexible than others in this regard. But if you are in a situation where you can't sell, let's say, one paintbrush company alongside another, so what? Go out and find a company that makes frames, another that makes easels, another that sells oil paints, another that sells watercolors…you get the picture.

- Vindication: I couldn't think of another word, but really, that's the best one (although "self satisfaction" comes close). If you're an entrepreneur at heart and are chomping at the bit while earning a salary, even if you love the overall business you're in, being an indie rep is a great way to prove it to yourself and your former associates that you are capable of making a go at it on your own. The same holds true if they have to lay you off—or worse, fire you! However, never burn your bridges—always bring your business contacts with you. If you're smart, you'll use them to establish stronger bonds in your rep relations, whether they are customer or vendor. Try not to be fired, though—that'll make it awkward should you try to deal with your former employer later as a customer.

(Remember, as an indie rep your most important asset will be your customer base.)

Always look at what your customers not only are buying, but what they can possibly sell to *their* customers. This kind of flexibility may take a company that uses an inside sales staff years to figure out and implement. As an indie rep, you can offer that kind of package more quickly.

Often, Indie Reps bring a varied background to the equation that a hired-out-of-high-school inside sales rep lacks. That's part of the payoff resulting from this freedom.

Of course, you could take "freedom" to mean you have more flexible hours. But if you are looking to start your own business with the idea of goofing off more often, you will fail.

Flexible hours should mean you work when you are best suited to get the job done. That may be late at night, early in the morning, or both, like Winston Churchill used to do, with a nap in between. If you are wondering, "How many hours a week will I work as an Indie Rep (or any self-employed situation)?" close this book right now, slither back to your boss with your tail between your legs, and ask for your job back. You will never succeed as an "independent" -anything, let alone Independent Sales Rep.

What kinds of people make good independent sales reps? Again, anyone with an entrepreneurial mindset often prevails. One must have an independent vs. dependent mindset. If you are in a job that you are constantly thinking you could have done better than the boss and events bear you out, you could be a good candidate.

If you are a buyer, store manager, or other decision-maker that sees a bunch of sales reps come through your door and you think you could outsell or outperform many of them, you could be a really good candidate—after all, you know how your future meal tickets already think.

You should also have a list of contacts in your given industry that would be willing to help you—both as vendors and as customers. You should know your industry well. Good independent reps are not car salesmen that shuck and jive you into buying a Lincoln, then drive home in a Chrysler. They should have some sort of industry experience. It's what you know, and it's whom you know.

I've been a representative in the entertainment/licensed products industry for more than twenty years. Before that, I was a buyer for a major chain of stores and a rack-jobber dealing in music, video, and books. I was fortunate in getting to know a few indie reps. I not only studied how they worked, but got to know them and had them share their expertise. When I decided to make the plunge into being on my own, a few companies I had contact with agreed to use me as a rep—with the agreement that whatever accounts I brought to the table would be mine, on a commission-only basis.

In spite of some stress-filled moments with my old employer, by the time I left I did not burn bridges—I was able to sell some things to my former company. In fact, I wound up making more in commissions selling to them, than I ever made in any position I had with them.

I was fortunate too in that the last week I was there, a company named Winterland advertised for sales reps in *Billboard*, the weekly trade magazine for the music industry. Winterland was the dominant player in their field and wound up being the best vendor I represented early in my career.

Remember what I said earlier about having the freedom to be flexible enough to add lines that suit your customers' product profiles. I already had several lines of music lined up, but Winterland really got my foot in the door of a lot of accounts, even though it was product that I really had not expected to sell when I started. And it proved to be the catalyst that enabled me to expand into other licensed products, which are the majority of what I sell today.

If I had stuck with a variety of music lines as I originally intended in the late 1980s, I would have gone out of business sometime around the mid-1990s when kids started downloading songs for free instead of paying $18 per CD to get that one song they liked.

I've noticed too that other indie reps I have met (and in some cases teamed up with) all share similar past histories. Being able to say to an account, "I know exactly what you're going through and where you're coming from," is powerful stuff—and will keep customers longer than the approach, "I know business is slow, but ya gotta buy this stuff now when it's hot." If you were a corporate buyer or store manager/owner at one point, you already know the inner workings of your customer/prospect's mind. If you are a habitually employed salesperson you may lack that advantage.

So if you are an inside sales rep who wants to go indie, keep that in mind. It may be worth your while to switch positions in the company you work with, from sales into purchasing or retail management, before you jump ship.

If you want to know why John Smith buys what John Smith buys, you have to see the world through John Smith's eyes.

Earn some time being as rounded a John Smith as you can be, even if it's just tagging along with another department for a week while you're still employed. I doubt any boss would object if you, as an inside salesperson, asked him/her, "I want to get a better feel for what Joe does in purchasing, and I was wondering if I could look over his shoulder for a few days I have free—would that be OK?"

Upon becoming an independent rep, it may take a while for you to really start earning serious money, but most indie reps consider a high five-figure or six figure income quite common. Get used to fluctuating incomes—some years will be better than others, particularly if your business is as fad-driven as mine has been. Get used to paying for your own health insurance, or at least going in on a plan your spouse has at his or her place of work. You will have to put together your own retirement portfolio. And get used to paying quarterly taxes. You may want to form an LLC or some other corporation. More on these aspects later.

Get used to deducting and keeping receipts/records for expenses in just about everything you do—that's another book entirely. You may be able to do everything out of an extra room in your home...and you should if you can get away with it! Author and consultant Alan Weiss estimates he was able to put his kids through college in the savings he made by working from home, while other consultants were renting fancy offices so they could have exotic signs and locales.

Weiss stresses that it's not how much you earn; it's how much you actually get to keep. Paying for a secretary when desktop computers rendered most of them obsolete twenty years ago is foolhardy. Pay for those things as you need them. (We'll cover basic necessities you need to start up later in the book).

But compared to other entrepreneurial activities (opening a restaurant, starting a software company, getting a retail store down at the local mall) setting yourself up as an indie sales rep is pretty affordable.

I will tell you this though; most, if not all, independent sales reps I know *love* what they do. They may want to augment their work to include other things, but I have never, ever known one that was even modestly successful who longed to go back to a steady paycheck.

As one rep told me before I left my old job, "If you want security, go to prison. If you want freedom, work for yourself—and there's no easier way to do that than being an independent sales rep."

There are reps I've known who are no longer around as reps. Many went into selling cars, real estate, or some other typical refuge of the habitual salesperson. If they enjoy that fate, more power to them. But I have a gut feeling they really wish they were still independent, working for dozens of lines instead of one, and making all the decisions. Circumstances, like lessening demand for the lines

they handled, territorial division, major accounts going un-
der/being sold/moving away, or other market factors, put
these reps out of business.

What I'll discuss throughout the book I hope will enable
you to avoid that fate...while making money and having
a lot of fun doing so.

CHAPTER 2

The Independent Sales Rep Process—
How It Should Work

In this chapter, we'll explore what you, as a rep ought to expect out of your vendors/suppliers, and what vendors ought to do to keep indie reps on top of things.

A. Communications

One of my early better vendor relations soured through no fault of mine, or really of theirs. They simply grew to a point where they no longer had a designated person who would keep me in the loop as far as new product was concerned. And they were using Fred Flintstone primitive technology in an increasingly George Jetson futuristic world. They did use the fax machine, which was pretty cutting-edge at the time, but rather than print out a report via some sort of computer program, they printed labels of the latest music releases they had obtained, stuck them on a sheet of paper, handwrote the quantities they had in LP, Cassette, CD, copied that, and faxed it to me. It was usually twenty pages worth of stuff, about two to three times a week and took the person doing it several hours each time.

And it would have been easily done today via email on one page of a Word® attachment or Excel® spread-sheet...with more vital information like price, UPC number, release date, etc.

I visited their offices one time and the managing director told me I was doing great, but I was "only as good as the information I was given." There's the rub.

Eventually, they had to cut me loose. They needed their personnel to upgrade their systems and concentrate on getting their label and imported product into bigger distributors, who eventually did the work guys like me were doing.

But I learned a valuable lesson. If a vendor cannot or will not keep an independent sales rep up to date, the rep is going to suffer for it. A rep doesn't want a customer stumbling upon a bit of information before the rep does. And vendors should have a systematic approach to keeping indie reps informed if they make the decision to use an outside sales force.

Technology today makes that easy, but you'd be surprised how many companies do it poorly.

Basically, communications with an independent rep network should consist of the following methods in any combination that best suits your product. And by extension, that information should get to the customer:

- Samples as needed so a rep can look and feel and then show to prospective customers.
- Print marketing materials like brochures, catalogs, sales circulars, so rep can digest and pass along.
- Email—in the form of announcements, newsletters, attachments (jpeg or PDFs please, no formats that are going to prove to be a pain in the neck for the average computer user). Make them regular—daily, weekly, monthly, whatever suits your industry. The rep should expect them.
- A Website—Who in the world today does not have a website? You'd be surprised. Anyone, and I mean *anyone*, should have one of some sort, no matter how small their business. Websites should act as a

destination for more detailed info promised in your email/newsletter communications. They can act as fill-ins between published catalogs, and the new release info should be easily printable so it can be added to an existing print catalog. They should be easy to read and use. Don't waste money on bells and whistles—just get to the point! And you reps out there who are checking out prospective vendors would be wise to be suspect of any vendor whose site just begs for a "skip intro" button, or has tons of info about picayune stuff like employees birthdays instead of new product. If their website stinks, chances are a lot of other things about them will too.

A rep's website can be as simple or detailed as he or she sees fit. I've seen some that have photos posted of every item in every line that rep group handles, with a shopping cart where the customer can order each item as he or she sees it, using a little blank box under said item. You may have to hire some Webmaster at a hefty income to put such a site together, but if you can do it, great.

A rep can set up a simple, economical website by basically making it a link to the rep's vendors' sites. An "order" feature can be added by having the Webmaster set up a page that includes a form for customers to fill out with their address, etc... and a text box where customers just type in the stuff they want while viewing the products on the different sites.

Again, though, this kind of site is only as good as the information it's given. If vendors allow their sites to go to seed, that can have an adverse affect, by extension, to the reps' site.

K-I-S-S: Keep it Simple, Stupid. Again, don't waste money on fancy animation, music, flash, etc. If you have to have a "Click here to enter" option on your home page, you've wasted your dough already. The home page ought to be limited to a few paragraphs explaining what the rep does—it should introduce those unfamiliar to the rep, and help navigate things for the rep's established accounts.

If you don't have anything of a sensitive nature, try to skip the password and user-name function. That's like handing a key to every customer of a brick and mortar store, and telling them the door is always locked, but they can use the key to get in. Guess how many would lose the key in that scenario? Worse, guess who'd not bother coming back, or at least resent it every time they had to pull out the key?

Most vendors have minimum order requirements or ask for tax ID Numbers when customers place orders. If you have such policies with your vendors, you'll easily screen out members of the public trying to get wholesale deals when they aren't qualified...so why bother with password and user name? Contact list, perhaps? There are easier ways...

You'll capture more useful contact names once you, the rep, have worked the leads you get properly.

In addition to the lines you carry, your site should have things like a new release newsletter, contact details (phone, fax, email), geographical details (if you handle a certain area)...that's about it. We'll cover this later in the book.

B. Support

Anyone deciding to go the indie route when it comes to being a sales rep had best understand that he or she is going to be on his or her own for the most part. A company uses an independent rep so it can get results with a minimal amount of effort and expense on their part. We've already discussed the need for steady communications and a supply of sales materials and samples. Other than that, the rep should be able to make things happen on his or her own in most cases.

There are exceptions, however. In situations where a line is being introduced to a major account, it may be a good idea for a rep to invite one of the principal staff members (like an owner, sales manager or sales VP) from the vendor to accompany him or her into the first sales meeting with the account. This is also a good idea when the vendor's relationship with the account may need some kick start, if it has something new and exciting to present, or if the vendor's staff member has just not met anyone at the account before and the rep would like them to meet face-to-face.

Another support aspect that should be considered is the rep-vendor relationship regarding trade shows. The rep ought to be able to get all the info he or she needs from the vendor prior to the show so that he or she can bring by customers during the show and be able to update that customer thoroughly. This can be done with a general meeting with the reps on the day before the show, or with a brief one-to-one meeting between rep and vendor. Vendors should make it a point to possibly schedule meetings with the rep and his or her customers if needed.

There are times when the rep needs help and has to call the vendor's office to get a question answered or some other need fulfilled. This is where the rubber meets the road when it comes to the relationship between vendor and representative. It's something like the relationship between a soldier on the front line and the HQ tent a few miles from the front. Good vendors will get the problem solved quickly and allow the rep to get back to what he or she should be doing—selling. Lousy vendors will, well, create a bigger problem.

What follows are a few examples of what to do and what *not* to do as far as vendor/rep support systems.

Every company invoice I've ever seen has some sort of notice that if an order arrives shorted (product charged for but not received), damaged, or with any kind of mistake, the customer should report it back to the vendor within a certain amount of time—usually 10 days or less. At one time I had a vendor who was notorious for sloppy service. Orders were not only routinely late (they averaged a four- to six-week turn when two weeks was the industry norm) but often poorly filled (customer got way less than what was ordered) and had a higher-than-normal proportion of shortages, misships and damages due to poor order packing or other production faults. I would get a call from a reliable customer who was reporting a shortage—doing their part as far as the invoice instructions were concerned.

Then I would relay that information to a fellow I'll call Lothar. Lothar would then proceed to argue with me on the issue and ask me to call back the customer and ask him or her how much the carton weighed because if it weighed what the vendor's shipping department said it weighed when it left their dock, the customer was lying and Lothar would not issue credit for any shortage.

This happened more than once with Lothar. As a matter of fact, it was usually the standard operating procedure with him. I don't know if it was *his* policy or his company's policy, but I have to wonder just what they were in business for if their prevailing attitude toward their customers was accusing them of reporting shortages on a few scant items just to rip the vendor off.

I do know the results were pretty consistent on the customers' side of the fence. Many customers wound up hating this vendor's ever-loving guts!

This is not the kind of support a rep needs. Remember, an indie rep relies heavily on his or her relationships and trust between rep and customer.

The worst thing a vendor can do to an independent rep is to make him or her look like a liar, fool, or scoundrel, to the customer. This bears repeating: The *worst* thing a vendor can do to an independent rep is to make him or her look like a liar, fool, or scoundrel to the customer.

Vendors that do this may as well employ a staff of snotty nosed kids fresh out of reform school to handle their sales duties. Reps that rely on such vendors are going to spend their time doing many more things than selling. Unfortunately, those many more things make these reps *no* money.

Now let's look at the right way to do support between a rep and a vendor.

Another line of mine sells a variety of posters and other art. The vendor has had its share of bumps in the road, but it always gave the customer the benefit of the doubt when it came to complaints about shortages or damages and corrected the problem quickly.

When placing orders with this vendor, it is rare that I hear anything more about the order until I get paid for it. It is rare that I have to call them and ask, "Where is that P.O. I turned in for so-and-so a month ago?"

By the way, that is important for a rep to remember—always give your best efforts to vendors to whom you can turn in orders and never (or rarely) have to worry about those orders again until it comes time for customer to reorder, or time for you to be paid. For the most part, you are being paid to make sales, not be a babysitter.

When this vendor noticed a higher amount of misships on two particular items (let's say stock number AB535 and AB939, since verbal orders via phone tend to make "five" and "nine" sound the same) they sent out a message to reps recommending that they write in the title or artist of an item next to the stock number to clarify it, when possible (AB535 Picasso, AB939 Van Gogh—so that when they see AB535 Van Gogh they *know* something is wrong and correct it).

When introducing new products in their line-up, this vendor allows any reps to ask to have a few samples sent to select customers or prospects that would likely be ones to benefit from such new product.

They introduced custom labeling for any customer who wants it—even if it is a small shop. This kind of service is usually reserved for large chains.

Any call into their office is either answered right away by a real person or returned within a few hours. Emails are answered promptly. Misships, damages, or shortages, although appearing far less frequently, are handled with, "We'll take care of this," and you know what? It *is* taken care of. Nothing is more comforting to a rep than a problem that goes away forever.

That's what reliable support is all about. A rep should shoulder most of the burden, but when he or she does occasionally need help, it should be prompt and efficient.

One other anecdote: A vendor of mine once had a support staff member who sent me an email asking about two P.O.s from one major account. Both had the same item on it—seventy-eight pieces on one P.O., thirty-six pieces on the next. The P.O.s were generated by computer, as most major accounts are prone to do. The support member asked me if it was OK to combine the total and stick it on the first P.O.

I went ballistic. They had just overcome problems in the past of improper procedures like this that resulted in the account not paying the vendor correctly since the invoices were screwed up—orders were over-shipped. And since some P.O.s were never being filled, they would ask us to clean up backorders to fill those P.O.s, all this while asking for returns for the extra amounts that came in on the invoices that were over-shipped.

Human beings get this—but computers don't. The first P.O. says ship seventy-eight. The next says ship thirty-six.

The computer identifies them with two different Purchase Order numbers. Accounting says: Pay for invoices that are accurate, and have assigned P.O. numbers properly.

I asked this support member to think about what she just suggested and get back to me. Her boss got back to me saying she was upset, could I please tone it down? I did, but I made my point. A customer gives you a "Purchase *Order*," not a "Purchase Request," or a "Purchase Pretty-please." Last time I checked, when one is given an order you reply "Yes Sir!"

Anyway, this support staffer did not last with this vendor. They took the high road, happily, and continue to be a most supportive line.

I'm not out to make some so-called support-staffers' life miserable or to get them fired. But if they are out to second guess the indie rep's efforts, to treat customer complaints with suspicion, to ignore the "ship to" column on an order, and have it sent accidently to a "bill to" address—and then make the rep out to be the villain, then they really should not be in the business they are in.

One other aspect of support that I find is usually a culprit, and not an asset to a vendor, are Rules. If the president or CEO of a company loads the support staff with a bunch of rules that the customer has to follow, that usually leads to trouble. John Wanamaker may not have been totally correct when he said, "The Customer is always right," but he certainly had the right idea. The guiding principal should be to retain that customer as much as possible and to help the independent sales rep retain that customer as well.

It's not uncommon to find situations where an employee is sticking to some interpretation of some rules that has the customer totally irate, and the rep is caught in the middle. If one were to get the boss who invented the rules in the first place in on the fracas, he or she would no doubt side with the customer and avoid a scene being made/ customer being lost.

Minimize the rules for your employees—and for your reps. Principles are better than rules and are easier to follow. Also, the more cumbersome you make things on outside reps, the fewer orders you may get from them. If a rep has only a given amount of time, whom do you think he's going to sell for? You with your endless rules, or the other guy who makes it easy to write orders?

C. Samples

Reps should have samples, and vendors should be prepared to deliver them if needed. Some companies charge reps for them—a practice I think is only needed should the product prove expensive or the rep needs more than their usual share. If a rep wants to get noticed by a major account, he should be sending some samples to the appropriate buyer, and the vendor should not make a stink about it.

Sending huge boxes of samples usually overdoes it, though. Keep in mind the rep may have multiple lines and only so much room in his car to carry samples around. Don't expect the rep to haul a steamer trunk around. Most customers and prospects are going to remember your product better if you are able to let the rep leave a catalog behind. Assuming an account will sit down and instantly write an order while looking through piles of samples is pretty antiquated. Small accounts are usually working with few people on the sales floor and they can't turn their attention away for too long. Large accounts have to enter data into their system before they can generate a P.O.

Best leave it up to the rep to request any more than basics when it comes to samples.

Depending on the nature of your business, you'll need a few or many samples to perform your job effectively as a rep. Some samples may be just for your own benefit (as a rep) so you can know precisely what it is you sell. This scenario presents itself particularly when you're dealing with something new and different. And, of course, you want to be able to show customers these samples or have them sent for them to discuss with their company.

The days of having to lug huge containers of samples may be coming to an end, or at least being curtailed quite a bit, thanks to the Internet where you can view top-notch photos of the stuff online. Having just a few samples of product and being able to show what colors are available via a website make the rep's job easier, no argument.

Companies should be ready and willing to provide samples to reps. In some industries, they charge the rep for them or maybe charge them if the rep decides to keep them after a given period, then issuing credit (thus voiding the invoice) when the product is returned. In most of my situations, I've been able to get samples free whenever needed, but I've really never needed them as much as others may have.

If a company does charge you as a rep for samples, it should be at a discounted rate. If you have a track record of selling a lot for a company, I really don't think they should charge you at all—for crying out loud, you're delivering results for them!

In some situations, you may find a company simply doesn't send samples. This may be because they figure customers are savvy enough to *know* what an ABC Gizmo looks like and they know the quality already. Honestly, does a Coke® salesman need to give a can of Classic Coke® to anybody?

An example of my own in this regard is Zippo® lighters; I represent a line that's a Zippo® distributor. A catalog for Zippo® is fine, thank you...but a few years ago Zippo®

debuted their butane MPL series of multi-purpose lighters, and if there was any situation with them where I wished I had a sample this may have been it. Eventually they weren't needed since Zippo® is one of those rare companies whose reputation is so good you really don't have to show a sample to anyone...a catalog or marketing piece will suffice.

Another example of a company refusing to send samples, and this time it backfiring, was a fashion line I had of T-shirts and sportswear that tied into a particularly hot TV show at the time. The show did have a reputation, but the apparel was uneven from a quality standpoint. Some of the early print runs were quite good, but as the line gained in popularity, demand went up, short cuts were taken, quality suffered, and service did too.

You may be thinking, "Well, if you showed good stuff and they shipped the bad, you'd be screwed!" Quite true, but there were certain designs that were pretty consistent and a savvy rep could have focused on those, perhaps showing good and bad styles side by side and asking the customer to focus on the safe ones.

This was a line that also did a poor job of printing catalogs and marketing material; they did not even have a website for wholesale purposes until it was too late. Reputation can only take you so far—if you don't follow up on it as a vendor you won't last long, and this line didn't; even though to my dying day, I think they could have become a long-lasting line, provided they played their cards right.

D. Catalogs and Other Marketing Material

Speaking of which, we come to print catalogs and other marketing material like brochures, flyers, etc. With the Internet, a lot of vendors are thinking they can forego this expense. Big mistake. There is still no substitute for some sort of print catalog for *any* company. I don't care what you sell if you are a vendor.

If you are a rep, be wary of vendors that can't understand this.

Put yourself in your account's shoes. Most of these may be small retailers. With minimum wage/taxes/expenses the way they are, they may not have unlimited hordes working for them, and they may have to manage the store alone during the hours you either call them or visit them. You may tell them about a website (which they may visit but often forget to) or you may have stopped by and shown them some samples.

These store owners/buyers/managers (usually the owner is all three) have eight billion things on their mind. If you think the owners will stop everything and order right there, guess again. Even if they do, they will just scratch the surface. I guarantee you they are wishing to do it later, or spread out over time so they can devote full (or better) attention to it.

If you leave behind a souvenir of your visit, or mail the owner a souvenir of the phone call you made, you give the owner the opportunity to do precisely that: put together an order when the owner is ready and when *he* or *she* can devote full attention to it. That souvenir is a print catalog or brochure.

Websites may be up to date, but can a computer be rolled up and put in a back pocket while Mr. Storeowner waits on his customers the way a catalog can? (iPhones don't do it, sorry—maybe someday, but not now). Is Mr. Storeowner willing to bring his customers behind the counter or in the back room to view your vendor's (or your) website? Don't count on it. But he can plop a copy of the catalog on the counter and show the customer your items, maybe asking, "Hey do you like this? Think it'll sell?" And from experience I can safely say they do.

Let's revisit that vendor that had T-shirts tied into the popular TV show we discussed under "Samples."

Motorcycle shops were good customers for me, but some of them wanted more details, more info. The website, late as it was, was poor—the photos didn't do the product justice, and those interested did not get all the info they needed. But to make matters worse, there really was no print catalog for the rep/vendor to give the wholesale account (i.e., the retailer).

We were given a publication, but it was more of a coffee-table book for the end user/consumer on the street. It had no wholesale prices, did not have any info on sizing availability, and was poorly organized. It was just a bunch of cool photos of guys and gals wearing the stuff with little captions telling what items they wore (but *no* SKU numbers! *Impossible* to order from!). Another impediment this "catalog" had was that it was odd sized (12"x12"—try finding a mailing envelope for that) and it weighed over one pound—a trip to the post office each time you wanted to mail one, due to anti-terror restrictions.

One of my bike-shop/motorclothes prospects had picked up a few basic apparel designs by this vendor via a distributor, had done well with them, and now wanted to step up to the plate and do some real ordering from the vendor via me. He wanted a catalog...and I had nothing to give him.

He told me he could "spend five hours online" looking at the website and taking notes, which would "keep me off the sales floor away from my customers"—*not* something one does in retail especially today when it gets more expensive to hire extra help. However, with a print catalog he could have knocked an order out in thirty minutes. He could wad it up into his back pocket and check stock against it. He could show it to his customers and get feedback from them (he wasn't about to let them into the back office to show them the same images online).

So print catalogs still have value. Every time I mail a packet of catalogs to each of several hundred accounts, I make back the expense within days—and these catalogs will last months, if not close to a year. Not all of my vendors participate in this activity, but it's pretty obvious that those who do have me writing far more orders for them.

Catalogs still have an allure that a website never will have...if they are well crafted and presented. At a convention/trade show an account of ours held one time, my associate David and I had made up a bunch of envelopes stuffed with appropriate print catalogs. As the first customers milled past our booth, we tried handing them out without saying anything. There was little response, since many had to fly home after this event, and they might have dreaded lugging more stuff home. Then we said, "Would you like some of our catalogs?" We got a better response. But then David started announcing, "Here's a *Gift Pack* that contains some of our catalogs, which might help you learn more about our product once you get home." Bingo! We got rid of all the packets within an hour. This also illustrates the value of "spicing" up a presentation—see how "gift" just *sounds* better, and appealing?

I'm still in touch with a former customer that continues to dabble a bit in the business and buys old samples from me on occasion. He came over once when I had my entire office floor laid out with envelopes being stuffed with catalogs for eventual mailing. He asked, "Do you have any idea how much everyone in our store went nuts whenever those catalogs arrived?" Of course I did—I usually got some nice orders from him. But it was good to hear this from him.

Vendors should have plenty of catalogs to let the reps use, and a good rep will use them. When a vendor establishes a relationship with a rep, the main thing the rep brings to the relationship is a roster of potential customers, prospects and leads that the vendor *doesn't have.* If the vendor gets stingy in the amount of catalogs the rep will be given, what is the wisdom of that? Reminds me of the old Yellow Pages TV spot where the carpet salesman declined on buying a Yellow Pages Ad, because the name of his business was "Sam's Rug"—not "Rugs", and "If I place an ad I may end up selling the only rug I have, then I wouldn't be 'Sam's Rug' any more."

If a Vendor gets 5-10% response from a catalog mailing, that's pretty good...ask anyone in the Advertising industry. And you never know how long it takes for a customer to finally bite. This is all basic marketing. So the independent rep should see to it any of his prospects that could conceivably sell a particular vendor, should have that vendor's catalog or print material. And the vendor should listen up when the rep asks for enough catalogs to accomplish this.

A good catalog should:

- Show the product cleanly, plainly, and clearly and in logical order. Group by product category or how a customer will likely want to refer to products. If your catalog is for timepieces, put desk clocks all together, watches in another section, etc. An index or table of contents is great.
- Give the ordering info under each item—this includes sku#, UPC, color, size options, other minor variations.
- Show Prices, but it's sometimes a good idea to publish a price list and stick it in an inside cover flap or put it in the back of the catalog. Retailers don't want their customers to know their wholesale prices.

Reps: Don't forget to staple your card to the catalog so the account knows whom to call when they have an order ready. A contact info sticker or stamp prominently placed will work too.

For about 100 years, L.L. Bean® has led the way in mail-order catalog sales, and for good reason. Their catalogs are in a Business to Consumer setting, true, but B2B (Business to Business) situations can learn a lot from L.L. Bean®.

L.L. Bean® publishes catalogs for different products and situations, and I don't know if this always works in a B2B setting. In my experience, I want most of my accounts to grow just the way my vendors may be growing, so if a vendor adds a new product line, I hope the customer does too—so I want the customer to get every category catalog a vendor has. But L.L. Bean® does put customers that bought from their Fly Fishing catalog on their mailing list for Hunting, Women, Camping, Winter, Spring, Summer, Bargains, and whatever other catalogs as well.

When you open any Bean catalog, it is laid out in a logical fashion so it's quick and easy to find what you need, even without the index. One Fall catalog I read had items for kids' back-to-school. A page featuring backpacks had the headline:

"The Book Bags That Sent The Competition Packing"
and arrows coming out of the photo of that book bag showing how it was clearly superior to other bags out there. An audio jack socket that eliminated worry about zipping through the cord was one I remember well. Put your iPod or radio in that pocket, plug the internal wire into your device, zip it up...then plug your earphones *out*side the pack.

The kids toting the pack were wearing L.L. Bean® clothes, of course, and arrows directed the reader to "Boots, Pg.42," "Jacket, pg. 75," and so on. Neat stuff, and among things that ought to be mentioned in a catalog page.

L.L. Bean® has a fantastic website; indeed, they were early to utilize one. But they still do print catalogs...they seem to have *more* print now than they did prior to the Internet—that says a great deal to the power of print marketing.

Think about how you, as a vendor, want to treat your customers, and by extension, your reps. Do you want ordering from you to be a potential hassle where they have to log on or put some disc in the tray? In a retail setting, being in front of the computer *could* be such a hassle. Or do you want the flexibility that print matter still affords?

Reps should give accounts something tangible to remember them and the vendor by, and something to make the customer's job a bit easier. Leaving them a catalog also creates a conversation starter next time the customer is contacted. If you ask them "did you look at that site?" they may say "yes," but how do you know? If you ask them if they got the catalogs you mailed, you can always know for sure by either tracking the package or asking them about certain things on the cover or on page 5 that they may find of interest.

A word on putting information on CD-Roms: as of this writing, I'm finding a few vendors doing this. It does not create the immediate results as print does, but it may do so in future. You *do* have to remind customers to actually look at them! Think about it: they open the package and can immediately leaf through a catalog or pamphlet. They see the CD and say "Neat-o," set it by the computer...and tend to forget about it.

They can be a good alternative for catalogs too heavy to mail in bulk, and attractive graphics on the label do help. They can also be a "lead generator" by cheaply drawing in a customer, getting them to respond if they want the larger print catalog. Just remember their limitation...in that they keep the retailer off his sales floor.

CHAPTER 3

What It Takes To Be An Independent Sales Rep

The skills required of an indie rep can best be broken down to four basics:

A. Entrepreneurial skills
B. Organizational skills
C. Persistence
D. Flexibility

A. Entrepreneurial Skills

It is crucial that anyone even thinking about becoming an indie rep has an independent attitude vs. a dependent attitude about everything he or she does in life. Take some of those personality tests if you like to see how you stack up. But realize this: you are going to be working for yourself.

You will be paid only for what you produce in the way of sales via commissions. No one, and I mean no one, will give you any pay for a slow day.

True, if you have twelve lines in your portfolio, you'll have to report to twelve bosses, but when you multiply the amount of people you report to, it is essentially the same thing as being responsible to no one but yourself. You should be harder on yourself than anyone else will be on you.

If you currently work for someone and are mulling over becoming an indie rep, here are some *good* signs that you will have a chance to be successful at it:

- You report to work on your own and work until a project is done...no one has to hold your hand to get you from one point to the next or from beginning to end. The project is not over when the clock strikes 5:00pm.
- You schedule your work well in advance and attack the tasks you've scheduled and relish checking them off when each is done.
- Whether your ideas are used by your boss or not, you constantly come up with new, different, and possibly exciting ways to do things for your company.
- You sometimes clash with co-workers when you implement some of these ideas on your own. You often wish you could work on your own terms.
- You can operate on a self-guided set of goals, rather than be given specific instructions by someone else.

I often think of "attacking" and "combating" scheduled tasks for good reason. Nearly every successful entrepreneurial type I have ever heard of writes down stuff to do and get done. They use "DayTimer" and "Outlook" and other paper and electronic scheduling tools, but they use much more—legal pads with things to do at certain times of day and check marks for tasks completed. If something doesn't get completed, they carry it over to the next day or at another time soon to be completed.

They *attack* the tasks they have to do, rather than fight them off. Time management is an offensive characteristic, not a defensive one. Entrepreneurial types are pro-active, not re-active. So because of this skill in time management, the successful prospective indie rep takes care of all his or her basic tasks (first two bullet points above) and has time to be creative (third and fifth bullet points above). The downside is dealing with sycophants and bean-counters who will work for someone else until the day they die, are fired, or retire, and they just don't understand your way of thinking (fourth bullet point above).

It's always hard leaving the nest—whether leaving home to go off to school for the first time or leaving that regular paycheck and the buddies at the office. But if you have confidence in these entrepreneurial characteristics, you are well on the way to becoming a successful indie rep.

B. Organizational Skills

A lot of this was covered in the last few paragraphs involving time management. There are loads of good business books on the subject (*One Minute Manager* by Blanchard and Johnson developed into an entire series of books). But organizational skills also cover things like the tools you use to do your job, the layout of your office, what equipment you will need, etc. These should go hand-in-hand with time management.

Will you be doing a lot of phone contact with your customers and prospects? Then get a reliable phone or phones—land line as well as cell phone plans. Shop a good deal as far as billing goes so that other things like high-speed internet access, a toll-free 800 number, fax line, etc., are all included, or as much as possible, on one bill.

Beware of any plans that say, "All you need is your cell phone, throw away the land line." Maybe technology will get us there some day, but I would rather pay a little extra a month if it means ensuring an account that can pay you $30K a year in commissions can get through to you without dropping out and communications are near flawless.

Have your phone, fax, copier, computer, etc., all within easy reach of your desk. If working out of your home, don't put your office near the kitchen, nursery, TV, etc. If you rent an office space, find an area that is *not* near construction, an airport, next to busy railroad tracks, or a swimming pool outside a modeling agency. Avoid distractions (although a radio or using the computer's CD/MP3 player may come in handy while you're catching up on paperwork).

Have things like copy paper, toner, and printer ink in supply. Customers aren't going to be too sympathetic when you say, "Oh, you sent me an order? Wait, I'm outta fax paper let me run down to the store, and you can fax it again to me in a few hours." Are you the kind of guy who's out of toilet paper when the hottest date of your life comes over for dinner? Of course not. Those slobs would never make it in our vocation anyway.

If you're working out of your home, don't get in the habit of working in boxer shorts or a robe. If you're doing that, you can't be taking your livelihood seriously. You never know when you may have to go out and see an account on short notice, go to the bank or post office to deposit a hefty check, or overnight some important package. If you're dressed already, you're ready to do those things.

Have things like catalogs and samples at the ready. When you discover a new prospect, be ready to send them or hand-deliver them a catalog/brochure that tells about the product you are selling to remind them of what you discussed with him as you leave. If you have samples, just show what's needed to give them an idea of what product you have to sell.

Don't try to lug everything under the sun with you on sales calls. Customers will roll their eyes when they see a huge stack of things pile out of a steamer trunk—they are only giving you about an hour or so of their time. If you leave behind some literature like a catalog or brochure, give them some sort of website link on top of all that; that will impress the prospect/customer far more than a massive collection of samples that he may forget in a day or so.

The odds are good that a customer will not want to buy from you at each and every meeting or each time you call. They have budgets to meet and "open to buy" figures to maintain. If you educate them well enough and leave them with a souvenir or an offer that encourages them to learn more about your stuff, odds are they will buy from you at the time when they are good and ready.

Organize your time around the education of your customers and prospects. Orders will follow. This is important. Most people *hate* salesmen. But they love educators/teachers. Take a hint.

Some reps may find they have to visit their accounts, so they need reliable transportation—a late model car, either bought or leased. It should be big enough to haul what you need to carry to your accounts and comfortable enough to spend days in, if needed.

The hit-the-road reps are slowly disappearing with technology doing what it can do these days. Use of email, websites, web conferences, conference calls, etc., is making travel less important. A system and schedule using these electronic means of communication is the best way to take the place of climbing into the car and visiting the accounts personally, although early in your career as a rep you should try to see most accounts and markets first-hand.

We'll get into more details on these kinds of things later, but it is crucial you organize your environment around the education of your customers/prospects.

C. Persistence *and* D. Flexibility/Variety

These two last skills are time tested and may just be the oldest traits of successful sales reps. I don't know if anyone has ever written a complete history of sales techniques through the ages, but I can see how the first two we covered (Entrepreneurial and Organizational skills) are traits that evolved as we see them today, over the last several hundred years. Persistence, Flexibility, and Variety, however, I see when I encounter the most elemental sales situations like carpet salesmen from the Near East, or carts/stalls/hawkers in markets or bus stations in Southeast Asia.

Sun-Tzu and Clausewitz have their fans, I know. But no better book has been written on sales and marketing skills than Dr. Seuss's *Green Eggs And Ham*. This is the story, of course, of pesky Sam-I-Am and his attempt to get the other guy (who looks kind of like the Cat In The Hat) to try a platter of Green Eggs and Ham.

He mixes persistence with a varying marketing approach—try them in a boat, or try them on a goat, in a box, or with a fox. The prospect is finally worn down and ends up trying (and actually liking) Green Eggs and Ham. The impression is given at the end of the book that he'll be a repeat customer...*very* important! Indie reps live for reorders.

That's the slight flaw of Dr. Seuss' book, by the way. The customer is *worn down*, when he should have asked Sam-I-Am (or rather, Sam-I-Am should have offered) to put him on his mailing list, with messages full of testimonials and other real-life situations describing what goes perfectly with Green Eggs and Ham. But, after all, it is a kid's book, and the good Dr. had only so many pages...

In real life that is how successful marketing works. Educate the customer with a scheduled set of calls, emails, mailings, faxes, etc. A sales rep then just cleans up when the prospect finally decides to become a customer (in other words, coughs up the dough and gives the order).

A successful indie rep must think in terms of being a successful marketer. *Marketing is your preparation of prospect's mindset and facilitating his thought process, so that when he becomes ready to buy,* you're *the one he'll buy from.* Think of your own purchasing decisions. Don't you want to make the best decision possible? Do you *always* buy based on low price? If you do, you probably get burned a lot. Your curbside must be filled with throw-away stuff that you return to the cheap-o store to replace regularly.

I notice indie reps that have failed over the years are those that approach every contact with the customer with the "Are you ready to buy yet?" approach. The customer's answer to this is usually similar to "That Sam-I-Am, that Sam-I-Am, I do not like that Sam-I-Am;" in other words, "Not just no, H*#@ NO!"

This type of rep may be persistent, but he fails because he is a poor marketer. He's not telling the customer anything the customer has not already heard. And the customer or prospect, unless he told the salesman to bug off on day one, often *wants* to learn more. So you must *vary* your approach by being flexible; give the customer some new information.

It helps having product lines that have a consistent schedule of new releases, sales, or other goings-on so that you *can* tell the customer something new and different to keep them continually educated. Have something fresh to tell the customer—don't just keep repeating page one of *Green Eggs and Ham.*

I learned this almost by accident *before* I was an actual salesman. When I was employed as a buyer for a music distributor, I was responsible for buying slightly-out-of-the-mainstream music like cutouts (bargain priced overstock or deleted albums), imports, and independent label releases. I was given my own catalog to maintain, and this catalog went out to the stores monthly. I also had a company newsletter column to write weekly, to inform the stores of news that happened between catalogs (and to inform them of what the next catalog would bring).

Remembering how I spent my adolescence pouring over the cutout bins and import racks at record stores, and how this was a great way to meet others that shared my passion for such musical goodies (especially if they were girls), I decided to put that passion in a catalog cover sheet, and rather than just give a laundry list of what was new each month or each week via the cover sheet or newsletter column, I was going to write reviews and essays to put forth my passion and pass it on to the stores. And I hoped they would pass it on to their customers.

It must have worked. I tripled sales for that department in the first year I had the job. And I was finding everyone from store managers to advertising execs who got our newsletter, to label honchos in Los Angeles, calling me, meeting me at parties, etc., and sharing in that passion, even if they weren't paying customers!

Persistence without Flexibility and Variety in your approach is like yin without yang...like, well...Green Eggs without Ham. Or, more accurately, like reading the first few pages of Dr. Seuss' book over and over again.

My Mother bought us a beautiful rug on a trip she took to Turkey a few years ago. She had the man who sold it to her ship it directly to us in Texas. As a result, he had our contact info. And within a few years, I guess he got successful enough to travel to the US on occasion to try to sell more carpets and rugs.

He would call me every six months or so and ask if I would like to come to the World Trade Mart in Dallas on such-and-such a date to see more of his rugs. I had told him from the start that this carpet I got from my mother was doing its job nicely, thank you. But he persisted with the same sales pitch each time, every six months.

He might have had better luck had he asked me for referrals or told me about some *other* kind of product he carried, like towels—I don't know—he never told me anything more about himself other than that he sold my Mom our carpet and would we like another one? In other words he was guilty of persistence, without flexibility and variety.

When I went to Indonesia to get married, I'll never forget the array of people selling everything everywhere I went, lining the streets with oxcarts laden with ice cream, soup, fried chicken, you name it, walking up and down aisles of trains or buses.

My best man and I were sitting on a bus waiting to leave Malang, the town where we got some official paperwork done prior to my wedding. Before the bus started back to my wife's town, hawkers selling water, soft drinks, fruit snacks, and newspapers came on board to sell to travelers ready for an hour-plus bus ride.

The newspaper seller shoved a copy of the Indonesian-language *Jawa Pos* at me, beckoning me to buy. My best man explained to him, in Indonesian of course, that I did not read the language and barely spoke it. The paper seller said something else to my friend, who politely dismissed him.

After the *Jawa Pos* seller left the bus, I asked my best man what the *Pos* seller had said. "After I told him you did not read Indonesian, he asked *me* to buy the paper, and then to read it to you," my best man explained.

Had the salesman still been on the bus, I think I would have forked over the Rp 500 (pennies in $US) just to reward him for his creative use of varying the sales pitch.

CHAPTER 4

Supplies And Setup Needed

This chapter will cover what you need to get started. You may be fortunate enough to find a partner and, between the two of you, you can raise enough money to rent a huge showroom with all the computers, copy machines, sample fixtures, etc., that you need for years to come.

But chances are you may not be that fortunate. And chances are if you try any of that *alone* you'll find yourself in a sea of red ink and be out of business soon.

The great thing about being an indie rep is that you can start modestly and work your way up as you see fit. The great thing about a company hiring an indie rep is not only do they *not* directly have to worry about expenses, they really don't want to hear *indirectly* about them either. The rep's financial woes are no business of the vendor unless the vendor partnered on a financial scheme with the rep, and those cases are rare.

The Demise of A Large Rep Group...
How Getting Big Doesn't Always Mean Staying That Way

You may find during your career that you come into competition with huge rep groups that are a constant threat to your existence. You'll marvel at their huge showroom, staff of support people and an army of sub-reps, while you sweat it out of your home office. But if you keep your setup, supplies, alliances, and business as simple as it can be for the job you want to do, you can compete and succeed against any other larger group.

One of the biggest groups in my business progressed over the course of twenty-five years to the point where they had to have control over the lines they carried, so they set themselves up as a distributor by buying their vendor's lines outright and re-selling it themselves under a different moniker. This way, they could simply tell their accounts that there was only one source for this prod-uct—them—instead of a few dozen vendors they hap-pened to rep.

As they added accounts with this setup, they strove to add ever-bigger accounts, until they landed the biggest retail account of them all. This account bought some packages of calendars from this rep group and then kept them in their warehouses and Distribution Centers until October—far too late in the year to put out calen-dars for the following year in those kinds of numbers and expect any success.

This account asked for the rep group/distributor to take the calendars back and cancel the bill due for them. Astoundingly, this rep group complied, and it wound up putting them out of business. A cautionary tale—don't let any one entity dominate your business to the extent that if something goes wrong it will bankrupt or destroy you. Overextension will kill an established rep group just as easily as a rookie.

A. Location

For most indie reps, working out of a home office is the way to go. The commute is great—there is none! You can write off a bit of your home expenses on your income tax return (check with a tax planner on this). With most equipment nowadays very affordable and in many cases able to do two or three things at once (fax/copier/printer combos, computers themselves, multi-line phones, etc.) it makes sense.

Another trend in the last few decades that lends itself to home businesses is the average size of homes in the US. If you were born any time after WWII up to about 1980, I would ask you to go back to the home you grew up in and compare it to an average home for sale in your area now. Unless it has been expanded upon, the first thing you'll wonder is "How did we all fit in this house?" This means there is probably a room you can convert into a home office in just about any home built in the last 30 years.

Or...I see a lot of affordable small cottage or "studios" that can be built in a backyard. Maybe you can convert a cabana to do the trick.

If you are guaranteed twice (or more) of the commission income you will need to pay for rent in an office or showroom, and you find you absolutely have to have an outside office or showroom, then go for it. Likewise, if you're in a city that is the center for your particular industry and there is a sizeable district for showrooms or offices, again, go for it. (Examples: New York, Los Angeles, etc.) But this is an option you may want to grow into and wait until the time is right.

You may do just as well, if not better, exhibiting at selected important trade shows for your industry.

Renting an outside office is the same way, although if what you're selling requires any amount of samples to show off, I don't see why you wouldn't go for an actual showroom.

Think of this, though; you can probably put a kid through college with the money you spend renting a showroom or an outside office. Remember what I mentioned about Alan Weiss in Chapter One. If you can do your job from home, and the customers don't mind, then work out of your home for as long as you can.

B. Solo Or With A Team?

Most Indie Reps I have known like working alone. In the last chapter, we talked about what it is like working alone, and if you don't mind doing just that, do it. There are plenty of reps that make big money and can handle the tasks needed all by themselves.

There may come a time when you feel the need to find a subrep or partner in another city/industry segment that can enhance what you do by expanding better into that area or industry segment. We'll explore two possibilities: If your reputation gets some other rep to ask *you* to join *them*, or if you need to find someone to help *you* (or they suggest it). In short, either you will be the junior partner or senior partner. Depending on what you are willing to accept (you may end up equals anyway) here's what to consider:

If you get asked to join another rep in selling his lines and you turning some of yours over to him, be wary. Ask yourself: "Who's to benefit here?"

If you get any sense that you'll be the junior partner in the relationship, tell him "No." You did not become an Indie Rep to become an employee all over again. And you may have some lines that can greatly enhance the other rep's business, whereas his lines won't do you much good (he could already have other reps out there selling this stuff, so what can he possibly give to *you*?). *Stay solo* in this case. They just want to feed off of you.

Fifty/fifty splits are nonsense if you are doing most of the work and the "Senior Rep" is just sitting back and providing "support." If you do most of the work, you should get 60%-75% or better, of the commission.

If some other rep or rep group proposes a partnership with you that avoids these pitfalls I just described, ask them to provide a contract or other written agreement.

An arrangement where you are working as a subrep in a big group of reps may be good training for when you strike out on your own. But if you rely on such arrangements, you're really not much more than an employee. One would hope if you're reading this book you want to know how to call your own shots and be your own boss, not work for someone else.

What if you want to take on a partner or subrep to help you with your business? Think in reverse of what I just described above. Find someone who has experience—an existing rep that has some of his or her own lines already is ideal. If they have worked in retail or purchasing in your industry, that is also a plus.

If your lines can enhance another rep's business and he or she can do most of the work in a geographic area you don't cover, or in a segment of the industry you don't cover (but would like better penetration) this could be the perfect rep/subrep relationship. Maybe some of the rep's lines could help you too—he or she may not have been able to crack the territory or the type of stores you currently handle with ease.

Make sure to explain to any potential subrep that they will work for commission only (if they do most of the work, a 60%-40% split or 75%-25% split in their favor). I would advise that anytime you get a call from a subrep asking for an advance, I would not only *not* give it to them, I'd start looking for a replacement.

I made the mistake of hiring a subrep once who constantly asked for advances, never kept track of his orders (he kept no log of what orders he'd written and was therefore due payment on), and to make matters worse, moved every few months mainly because he kept getting evicted or divorced. This meant his phone number/fax number were constantly changing (this was before cell phones, but he would have screwed that one up too, believe me).

He had *no* lines at all when I took him on, and I was only able to give him a few lines, but good ones, because of territorial restrictions I had with the rest of my lines. He had to take part-time work to get some money, which I didn't mind, but then he complained he did not have time to do what I needed him to do because he was tired after his part-time job and needed to relax!

I made it plain to him at the start that what I could offer him would certainly get his foot in the door with other vendors if he wanted to pick up some more lines on his own…something he never showed any inclination of doing.

However, I did replace him with another guy who had some lines already and could possibly get my lines into accounts I had no knowledge of (he did get a few, but with the combination of my lines and his he was able to open more new accounts for both of us). This second rep never once asked for an advance, and if I gave him information about new product, often the only proof he got that info were orders of that particular product.

We eventually parted company because he got another gig selling non-competing but related goods. Instead of selling licensed apparel, he became a rep for a major apparel manufacturer that was looking for accounts that wanted "Name Drop" on their polo shirts, T-shirts or caps—corporations looking for uniforms, etc.

Guess which one I'd hire back if I ever had the opportunity? Again, if you are an *independent* sales rep, look for someone else who is *independent*.

Go back and re-read the last chapter on what kind of person makes a good, independent rep, and look for someone who shares those characteristics.

In concluding this section on forming partnerships, other factors need to be considered: things like age, sex, ethnicity. Those can and do count. If I am an ugly, over fifty, white male, and one of my companies decides to delve into product that fits in real well with the young-women's urban hair-care market, a subrep who looks something like Halle Berry or Beyonce Knowles may be exactly what I need—provided of course she meets the other properties we discussed—has other lines, prior experience in retail or purchasing, etc.

C. Support Staff? Or Not

Some of you may find the need for help in answering the phone, clerical, bookkeeping, etc. This is entirely up to you but, like renting an office or showroom vs. working at home, consider how much you can save if you do it yourself. If you absolutely don't have the time and have exhausted all avenues to make these mundane chores easy and quick, then hire someone part-time first, full-time later. Some of this may very well be outsourced.

You should definitely have someone outsourced to do your taxes. Stories abound of the IRS going after self-employed types who make a lot of money and for good reason. If you have someone else doing this for you, they should (and will) back you up in any audit situation with the IRS if they have any reputable qualities at all.

Of course, outside legal help is something to keep in mind. Forming an LLC or looking over contracts, is not something many reps can do on their own (the "easy-to-do-on-your-own legal forms you hear advertised on radio ought to be avoided). Not many reps can have legal counsel on staff.

Clerical or phone help is nice, but if you work out of the home, why bother?

Do not use answering services. This is such a stupid waste of money I am surprised anyone uses them any-more—or ever did. With the answering machine at least thirty years old, the *digital* answering machine fifteen to twenty years old, cell phones a common part of life for fifteen years...why on earth hire anyone to answer the phone for you and give you a message to call so-and-so back? I have always noticed that anyone who uses a service like this gets back to me later than someone who relies on their machine or cell phone, and with less of an idea on why I called to begin with.

In bookkeeping and general tallying up of your com-missions, again, hiring help for this is nice, but if you ask me, I want to know *exactly* what I am getting paid for, when, where, why, and how. I want to be familiar with how I stand on what orders I was paid for and what or-ders I was not paid for. I want to know turn times and fill percentages. You can get good computer programs that can do all this I'm sure, or you can just tally it up longhand like the days of old.

However you choose, you must keep records of any and all expenses, income and your profit or loss (hopefully profit) each and every month. Compile running totals for income each month and compare figures to the previous year. There are plenty of books and software out there on this subject.

I have seen and known many reps who simply get a commission check and put it in the bank without checking to see how the orders on the statement match the period they actually wrote them; in other words, were there other orders that same month that got left *off* the statement, and why? Always follow up on this or hire someone who *will follow up* on payments and orders. You'd be surprised how much you'd leave on the table.

If you have to hire someone as a staff member, there is one I recommend you hiring first—a receptionist and some-one to handle clerical skills. I'd do bookkeeping myself; and always have an outside tax advisor handle taxes.

But many reps go for years without such help, and once again, remember how much money you save (and keep) without such help if you don't really need it.

D. Supplies, Equipment

Things you should own or buy when you start your work as an indie rep—and just for fun we'll estimate costs (in parentheses):

- A reliable late model **car** (You can spend what you want, but a perfectly useful late model used can be $15K or less—and you can lease a decent model for $300/month or less). You need to get around. Period. And it should be comfortable enough to spend hours in, if necessary; plus it should be big enough for you to tote around samples and supplies for your accounts. An auto is only transportation—get only the ride you need. Late model used or leasing is frugal and smart. Spend your money on more important things, and pay attention to the quality of work you do.

- A reliable and late model **computer** ($1000 to $1500); as much as possible peripheral stuff, too, like a **printer** ($100-150), **scanner** ($100-150), **hard drive back-up** device (real important, yet few people have one–they cost $100-300; go with the best for your system requirements), **high-speed internet access** of course ($50-80 per month or less), **email** programs and sev-eral email addresses (Usually free with your Internet Service Provider, or packaged with a website) and **software** programs such as Office® (Word® document processor, spreadsheet program Excel®, Power Point® slide show program, and other useful programs, MS Office® runs about $500). You should have *common* programs that people use and communicate with now via email. Adobe® for PDFs is an example. Get a PDF writing program too, since some images like Jpegs can be memory-heavy and hard to send via email attachment. Several are available online and are free—just do a Google search for "PDF writing programs" (Primo PDF® is an example, and it's free). Many useful programs come bundled with a computer anyway, so you may not need to add much to what you have already.

- A **Website** or at least a domain name and host so that you can build later (anywhere up to $750 to set up and domain/hosting fees about $200 per year— shop around, though). A website with your own home page, contact info, and links to your vendors is a natural layout for a site for your customers to refer to. More of this is covered elsewhere in the book, particularly in Chapter 7.

- **Copy Machine** capable of 18+ per minute or better. Leasing is the way to go with copiers and you can lease a good one around $100 per month. Be sure you insure it too; it may not be covered under your homeowner's policy.

  Newer copiers can perform functions of scanning from your computer and fax machine chores. Leasing is a good option since copiers can be expensive, and when they need service it helps to have a maintenance agreement. Running off copies from your computer is OK for small amounts of copies, but the time may come when you need a lot, and fast. There is no substitute for a good copy machine.

- **Fax Machine** ($100 or less; some combo models will run more). I'm hearing more and more that email attachments and improved email programs, plus more sophisticated copiers, are rendering the good old fax machine obsolete. I don't quite agree—yet—but I may in the future. You can still get a cheap, reliable fax machine, sometimes in a combo with a copier/scanner. But the stand-alone fax is still a quick way to send copies of documents that don't need to be perfect—and in many cases in less time than it takes to scan, save, file, and attach to an email message should you do it via computer. It is also more secure than risking online communication, if you are sending info like credit card numbers. Get a separate line for your fax, too; come on, most phone carriers offer packages that make an extra line very affordable. I was tickled to find one of my accounts complaining about a competing rep that was obviously using one phone line to switch back and forth between his fax and his dial-up Internet access; the customer had so many busy signals she threw the order away. I know this customer's order potential, and chances are the order's commission would have paid for the $40 or so that any phone service would charge to set up an extra line. *NOTE*: services like "Efax®" are highly recommended. This service sets up a new fax number for you (you can call forward from your existing fax number so no need to tell everyone your fax number is changed) and all your faxes come to your email mailbox as PDF attachments, which are very easily forwarded to whomever you want and can be saved and printed as desired. Fax services like this are well worth their fee (under $20 per month).
- Of course, you need a **phone**. I recommend both a cell (Plans with a "free" phone can be had for $100/

month or less) and a landline (You can get phone, answering machine and caller ID, all for around $100 or less). This is your link to everything. These phone lines should be designated for business only. Nothing will frustrate you more than trying to reach an elusive customer and getting one of your daughter's friends cutting in on the call-waiting. Again, as with a separate fax line, if you can't see the penny-wise/pound-foolish aspects of scrimping on phone lines by multi-tasking them, you may fail in other aspects of this line of work. By the way, Toll Free numbers are easily obtained and can park on top of your existing numbers without interfering with them in any way. Even though most long distance plans pay for package deals instead of per call, it still looks good to offer your customer a toll-free number to get in touch with you. And the numbers are easy to remember. As for cell phones, between the time I am writing this and the time you read it, cell phones will have advanced so much there is little point in me explaining just how much they can do, and I will include Blackberry® type devices, too, here. They aren't just "phones" anymore; they are cameras, Internet portals, email devices, entertainment centers, and more. Let's sum up by stating that any phone or device that keeps you easily within reach of your work is a good idea. Nothing will infuriate your customers or vendors more than not hearing from you when you're needed. Another hint: set up any and all of your numbers on the "Do Not Call Registry" so you are not interrupted by telemarketers. It's *your* business line, not theirs. You can find out how online at www.donotcall.gov

- A good digital **camera** ($100 to $300—your choice as to how good a model). The cell phone camera will do in a pinch, but there may come a day when your vendor or customer may want you to document something via a good photo. A customer may benefit by you showing him or her how another store displays your goods, or a vendor may ask "Wow! They're selling a bundle of these. How are they displaying them?" You can snap a few shots, discard the lousy ones right there (couldn't do that back in the days of film), and keep the good ones. Then go home, download them to your PC, and send them off in an email attachment.

- You may find you need a good digital **recorder** ($100 or less) to document speech the way a camera documents visuals, but a lot of people may freak out if you ask to record them. Another thing to consider is a digital recording program on your PC, hooked up to you phone's speaker (programs you can download are as cheap as $30). Provided it is OK with those you record; in many states you must tell them up front you are recording. Check your state's laws on this. There are websites that may tell you what's legal and where. I've used this on rare but effective occasions when a customer is upset with a vendor and passing on the word to the vendor is not enough. Remember the motorcycle shop desperate for a print catalog? He approved my recording him, just to make his point. Hearing the rage or hurt in the actual customer's voice *is* effective, but this is optional.

So what does the ticket come to? We can start a rep business from home with the stuff you have to buy outright for less than $3000, but some of these things (computer, maybe your car) you probably already have! For your monthly payments (in addition to your expenses in mailing, travel, etc., you're looking at $400/month or less—$750/month if you're leasing or buying a car with payments. Note: these are 2008 figures.

E. Budget Concerns

Doing work as an indie rep, your budget will break down as follows:

- **Communications Expenses:** phone bills, Internet access (some plans bundle together). If a rep makes about 400-500 calls per month, that can average a $250 to $350 bill. This can combine an office line, toll-free service, fax line and cell plan. Internet access can be anywhere from $20 to $100 per month depending on what type of access you can get in your area—DSL, satellite, whatever. What about website upkeep, domain name, hosting fees, and search engine optimization? I was lucky to latch on to a brilliant student that designed and continues to maintain my site for a reasonable fee around $1000 per year. Domain/hosting fees can run about $50. Webmaster and Search Engine fees can run a bit higher but shop around.
- **Mail and Package expenses.** This fluctuates. I do two massive mailings per year of about $500 each, and figure about another $1000-1500 on top of that spread out over the year.
- **Travel expenses**—auto upkeep, gasoline, airfare, hotels, meals, etc. Everything you spend on anything when away from home. You may lease a car or buy it (see section on cars above). At this date in history gas is selling for $2/gallon, but was twice that four months ago—will it get better or worse is anyone's guess. Airfare is going to vary also, but if you fly a lot sign up for those frequency programs! Hotels can be a real waste of money—so called "budget" hotels can be just fine for what you need them for—a place to sleep and do a little work—insist upon wi-fi, plenty of electrical outlets, etc. I eat just fine on about $30/day or less—skip lunch unless you have to entertain a

client. Gordon Gekko (remember, "Greed is Good" from the film *Wall Street*?) had this one absolutely right: "Lunch is for wimps". It is a time- *and* money-waster and will inevitably make you drowsy for the rest of the afternoon.

- **Office or showroom** rent and other expenses if applicable. Doesn't apply if you work from home, but do discuss with your tax professional on how to deduct that percentage of space in your home you use for work.

- **Subrep's** share of commission—slightly different from paying a staff member since you don't have to deduct taxes for a subrep; they take care of their own taxes just like you do. And the good thing about them is they are unpredictable in a nice way; you only pay them for what they actually earn in commissions, and you take your percentage off the top.

- **Promotional/marketing expenses**: do you advertise in any trade magazines? Website upkeep can be classified here, too. This is an important expense but, depending on the size and nature of your business, may vary from one rep to another. When advertising in the past I found $1000 for twelve issues in the classified section of a trade magazine pretty typical.

- **Taxes:** Even though they are really personal expenses, don't forget the taxes you must pay quarterly. Your state may also require income taxes be paid annually or several times a year. If you figure roughly 25% to send quarterly, you won't be too far off. And avoid (yes, avoid) paying too much where you get back a "refund" after you've filed your return. The Government is earning interest with your money when you overpay quarterly. Don't be afraid to pay a little less quarterly, but have money ready at the time you file in case you owe more.

You should already know what your personal living expenses are, and this is not the place to analyze those numbers. But I would recommend that when adding all items up in the points above, you should strive to earn *two times* or more of that total figure. Either find new lines to boost your income, or find ways to cut those expenses (or better, do both).

It's not just what you earn, it's what you keep.

F. Outside Support—Legal, Taxes, etc.

Every rep will eventually come to need outside support for a few facets of his or her business that he or she really doesn't want to tackle him- or herself. Taxes and Legal matters are two good examples of this.

I recommend you *don't* do your taxes yourself. I don't care how easy-to-use some of the software out there is. Paying a professional to prepare your returns is insurance and money well-spent. If you're reading this book outside of the USA, maybe all this doesn't apply, but governments being what they are, I'd be willing to bet you can some-how see how your tax laws may present you with a similar situation to how we do things in the USA.

With multiple streams of income from many possible sources, and the odds are that you are saving receipts for expenses in everything you do, you could very easily mess up your bookkeeping. The IRS often targets folks like you for audits, because they want to make sure you're paying all you should, quarterly as well as at the end of the year (actually, by April 15th the following year).

With a tax preparer, your returns look more legitimate, and even if you *do* get audited, any good preparer will come in with you and back up what you've presented. If the preparer has made an error, he or she should bear the brunt of the penalty you may be required to pay.

A good tax preparer will also alert you to every de-duction or refund you are entitled to. Try to avoid the big tax-prep outfits that advertise how many thousands of returns they handle. You want someone that'll pay better attention to *you*. A real tax service professional or a Certified Public Accountant is really the way to go and they are worth the extra money you'll pay them.

Speaking of insurance, that's another thing you want to be sure you're covered on. If you work out of your home, your homeowner's insurance should cover any sort of damages that acts-of-God will do to your computer, copier, phones, files, etc. If you have a small office or showroom and a small staff, get whatever liability coverage you will need.

Legal help is another thing you want in your arsenal. Find a lawyer you can call on occasion if issues like collecting commission payments, problems with accounts, or other matters come into play. Lawyers specializing in business law would work best for you. I would strongly recommend any rep to incorporate or get LLC (Limited Liability Company or -Corporation) status to protect his or her personal assets from frivolous lawsuits—or heaven forbid, *legitimate* lawsuits! Fees for incorporating or forming a LLC can vary anywhere around $1000, but again, think of it as insurance.

Once you've registered with your state or local government under a specific corporate or LLC business name you will have that moniker as long as you want. Your letterhead, business cards, listings in directories, all that stuff, should use that name. Your business expenses should be paid from a checking account using that name.

Find a good financial advisor too. You're responsible for your own retirement now—no one is paying your pension except *you*. Save via an IRA, or SEP.

Take time to protect yourself. Would you really want to risk all you have to things like IRS-taxes-owed hell, tornado, hurricane or earthquake damage, a spiteful employee, or a customer who wants to sue you as well as one of your lines for some real or imagined slight? Imagine trying to close the deal of your life in the future, and something like one of these nightmares comes out of left field! Get these things that are legal-, tax-, and insurance-related taken care of so you don't have to worry about them should any of them pop up.

CHAPTER 5

Matching Vendor Company To Rep

As a rep, once you have started your trade as a salesman, it will be important to add as many lines—vendors—as you can handle. It'll be an ongoing process; in effect, you'll need to market yourself in ways to bring those new vendors over to your side—much in the same way you sell to your customers, you'll have to sell yourself to potential vendors you wish to represent.

What's the most important item you have in your possession as a rep? In other words, if your house was about to be hit by a tornado and you had one thing to take with you from your office before you ran outside and down into the storm cellar, what would it be?

It's your client list, your customers (your Rolodex®, or however you have it listed). You really shouldn't have it exclusively in a hard drive of a PC. Make it semi-portable as in a pocket organizer, Blackberry®, or the good old-fashioned Rolodex®. This will be the thing that will help you attract the second-most important item:

The portfolio of lines you're selling.

Most books I've found that cover the subject of being a sales rep strictly cover the relationship between the rep and the customer. They assume that the rep who picks up the book already has a stable full of vendors to represent and sell for. That may be so, but I doubt it. In nearly every business, a multi-line independent rep is going to be adding lines all the time, and they *should*.

There may be a few books out there designed for the corporation's use in finding the right outside reps. To be honest, the ones I've found that approach our subject from this angle are pretty pricey. I'm hoping that those in a corporate setting that want to know how to find a rep will find this volume a bit more affordable!

Now, how do reps and vendors discover each other?

A. Trade Shows

Most industries have at least one, often more, trade shows and, at any of these shows you'll see signs out in front of any given booth saying, "Reps Needed." If you're a vendor, this is a good idea, since you'll want a rep experienced enough to be attending the show in the first place. If you're a rep, take this approach:

Go into the booth. Flip your name badge around so they don't know what or who you are at first. Act like a possible customer and see how you're treated. This is *very important*. Ask for a catalog or some sort of marketing materials...again *important*! If you haven't gotten the idea up to now, I'll state it again. An incompetent vendor is going to be more trouble than it is worth in many, many cases.

If the vendor is truly busy, and that is a good sign, it's OK to come back later. But eventually, you'll want to strike up a conversation with them and let them know you're a rep. If they have a sign out front saying they need reps, ask them if your territory or field of expertise (for instance, you service only grocery chains or drug stores) is available.

If they don't have a sign, simply ask if they use indie reps and, if so, is your area/field available?

Be armed with plenty of updated résumés when you attend trade shows. More on what a résumé for a rep should look like later this chapter.

Often at trade shows, there may not be time to have a detailed "sit down" interview to feel each other out. That's what the résumé is for. Exchange cards and arrange to call each other when you get home, or you may even be able to talk a little later at the show.

Unless you're good and familiar with each other already from past reputations, don't cement any relationships until you've had time to check references, ask around, etc. The great thing about a trade show is that there are plenty of possible references right there. If you're a rep, ask other reps you know from around the country, "What's this line like—easy sell or hard? Do they pay on time? Is their accounting good? Fill rates, turn times?" etc.

If you're a vendor, the rep's résumé should have other lines that he or she is selling and they may be exhibiting right near you. You may not want to ask some other line that is competing with you closely, but if there is another line that sells product that complements yours well and is not in direct competition...bingo! That's one to ask, "How is this rep? Do they get results? Are they able to sell without asking for tons of samples? Are they always hounding you for money? Do they keep their own books well?" There are many such questions.

B. Published Guides and Directories

At trade shows there are usually booths with agents from publishers of industry-specific guides and directories that match reps to vendors and vice-versa. Other guides match vendors to accounts and present other relationship leads-building situations.

Become familiar with them and see the appendix at the back of this book. Here's the great news for you reps: many of these directories publish rep info/résumés *free* of charge, and they will update your listing yearly—again, *free* of charge.

Here's the bad news for you vendors looking for reps: you're the one who foots the bill for these guides. But they are usually worth the $100 or so, especially if you are a company that may have to hire reps to handle different types of business.

Let's say you have a company manufacturing collectible figurines and tabletop statuettes for decorative purposes. You have had success in gift shops, but you now find some of your statues are weatherproof and are being sold to customers in those same gift shops that are putting them outdoors on patios, in gardens, etc. Your existing rep force has absolutely no relationships with accounts that can carry you in that direction—lawn and garden centers.

By using these guides, you can find reps that call on Home Improvement, Hardware, and Garden Center stores. The guides will be able to indicate where each rep specializes and in what industries they are most established. And the guides are usually conveniently divided into geographic regions, making it even simpler for a vendor to find where he or she needs help.

I've been flabbergasted over the years at some of my fellow reps that have *thrown away* the surveys these publishers mail out each year. There is no doubt most of my lines have come to me by referral or industry-related word-of-mouth, but I have had some nice lines yielding thousands of dollars per year that I latched onto *free-of-charge*, thanks to these directories.

Vendors using these directories are often new to an industry and have not built up a huge Rolodex® of contacts yet. Or they may just be expanding beyond their normal boundaries, either geographically or product-wise.

One of my best successes in this manner was a small, regional, custom screen printer who serviced the

Maryland/Delaware/Virginia area with T-shirts and other printed apparel. There was a talented cartoonist they were affiliated with who came up with a line of "Redneck Style" T-shirts. They featured a cartoon on the front of each shirt, like, "Firefighting Redneck Style." The cartoon featured four good-ole-boys peeing on a campfire with dozens of empty beer bottles strewn on the ground.

Each shirt in the "Redneck Style" series had a backprint down at the shirts' tail depicting the waistband of jeans and a butt-crack showing, complete with a personalized belt embossed with the name "Bubba" (this was long before this look became fashionable for young women, by the way).

The owners of this company had regional success with the line and wanted to take it national. They rightly assumed there would be other regions of the country where this would sell well. With slight modifications to the art on "Redneck Style" (Bubba wearing cowboy hat and boots instead of a trucker cap and sneakers), we were able to place this line in a major chain of discount department stores in the upper Plains states/Rocky Mountain states, and in a major chain of Western stores in the Southwest.

When they finally decided to go back to concentrating more on their custom work, we still had accounts wanting "Redneck Style," but this company had decided to finish with it. Still, it was a nice run while it lasted, and they would not have had found us without one of these published guides.

As a Vendor, you may be wondering, "Why buy one of these directory or guide books when I can find reps online?" and you're absolutely right.

C. Websites

Many of these published guides also have websites. They may charge a subscription fee for access to the site's database of reps. But isn't $100/year in a subscription to access one of these sites (where you may very well get the published guide *also*) worth a shot at $100K or so of extra business, like my friends at "Redneck Style" experienced?

As a rep, you'll find these sites also charge you *nothing* at all to post your résumé or profile. Again, look in the appendix in the back of this book for some of these, but just doing a word search for "Independent Reps" will give you a pretty healthy list of sites to use for the purpose of getting your name out there.

But if you are a rep, what about your own website?

If you don't have one, *get one now!*

If you do have one, find a way to *get noticed.*

We'll cover more on what your site should contain and how it should work later, in Chapter 7. But keep in mind the things that help customers find your site will also help potential vendors and other partners find your site. If I can leak out a bit of info early for the benefit of this chapter, here's something important on "getting noticed" on the web:

Make your home page tell as much about you in as succinct a manner as possible. Think about how someone is going to look for you. What are they searching for, where, why, when, as well as how?

Search engines like Google, Yahoo, Ask.com, etc. will match key words and phrases that you have on your home page with the words and phrases someone who's doing the searching will use. So, of course, you want to mention:

- Types of product you sell—in as plain a language as possible, but also in as many variations as possible. If you sell fishing tackle, words like angler, fisherman, rod, reel, spin casting, fly-casting, bait casting, lures, hooks, line, sinkers, and of course "Fishing tackle,"

should all be in your introductory paragraphs on your home page.
- The geographic area you cover, particularly if you're assigned a specific territory.
- Who do you sell to, wholesale or retail? Very important.
- What distinguishes you from your competitor?

The last entry will not be the type of thing that affects a search, but once a vendor (or customer) gets on the site, it *is* something that will make them take the next step.

Have your Contact info readily and easily available so the vendor (or customer) can call or email you to take the process one step further. Maybe not on the home page, but on the "contact us" or "about us" tab.

A site that enables your customers to link to each of your vendors is effective, yet fairly easy and cheap to set up and maintain. If a vendor were looking for a rep, wouldn't you think that would be important to them? It says, "Here are the lines I sell," and it assures that vendor won't be overlooked by everything else you sell as a rep, especially online, which is more and more important these days.

D. Referrals

One of the easiest ways to make contact between vendors and reps is one of the easiest things to forget... maybe because it is so easy. Just *ask*! If you are starting out and have just left a full-time job, try to leave amicably. Then, ask them, "Hey, I'm going to be selling companies A, B, and C as an indie rep, but I'm still looking for more lines, do you have anyone in mind? And if not, if you *do* find someone, here's my card."

Some of you may be fortunate enough to sell to your former employers because of the relationships you have there (again, don't burn bridges when you're starting out). But some lines may not allow you to sell your former employers since it may be a conflict of interest or they already have someone responsible for the account.

Here's why referrals are important. They may get you a line that *will* allow you to sell to your former employers. And more...

The field of Sales is still largely a relationship business: Like Breeds Like.

If someone knows and trusts you, they will recommend you to someone else they know and trust, figuring that "Like Breeds Like." But this process isn't always automatic. So *ask* for referrals.

The best time to ask any contact for a referral is when the relationship is fairly well established. If you've made some sales to an account you have a good track record with, ask them if they know any vendors who are looking for someone to help them boost their sales. If you've sold for a vendor for a while and have a good track record with them (and they've treated you well), ask them if they know of a company that is similar to theirs, but not in direct competition, that can use your services. You reps handling fishing tackle might ask your source of rods and reels if they know a manufacturer of polarized sunglasses or small boats/canoes to whom they could sing your praises.

A great time to ask a vendor for such a referral is after you've delivered a major account to them and put to bed the first big purchase order...or after you've spent a few months placing a lot of small orders, opening many new accounts. Certainly not earlier than that, but any time after that is a good time to proactively ask for referrals, as your time and workload dictate.

That leads us to the next question: What to do with referrals that call you and you can't handle them? As a rep you can take on as much as you possibly can stand, unlike other maverick-type professions like consultants, private detectives, etc. Those professions have to constantly look for the next job, since they really can only handle one or a few jobs at a time. In independent sales, there is much more room allowed for an "I can help you sell your stuff" flexibility.

But if you honestly can't take them on, explain to them that your dance card is full and there may be some lines that present a conflict (you need not distinguish between a conflict of time vs. a conflict of product lines), but you'll keep in touch with them as you never know what may develop.

I've almost *never* had a line that I've had to turn down unless it was for ethical or moral reasons. Remember, Like Breeds Like.

If some former acquaintance of yours is somewhat of a scuzzball and you get a referral from them or because of them, watch out. If the two are buddies, do you really want to deal with another scuzzball?

I had a vendor sales manager once who never settled at any one company long enough to make any sort of impact, it seemed. At one particular company I repped, he happened to be there when they had a product that was particularly hot at the time. I had an associate rep in the Kansas City area, but only the Kansas side, because of the territory this line gave us. Keep in mind: Kansas City sits on a state line.

The sales manager could not understand the slow sales this associate of mine was producing, but he failed to re-alize that there were reps from Chicago who were han-dling the Missouri side (which had more plum accounts) of Kansas City. So he fired my associate without first talking to me. The sales manager left this company not soon there-after. I never forgot this...

Particularly each year or two after that when he'd be at some other new company asking me to consider the line he was now working. Yet I noticed each one of his companies had a bad reputation—stupid product, lousy service, mistreatment of rep groups, etc. The last one he called me about (as of this writing) took the cake.

He left a "teaser" type of message on my answering machine saying he could hook me up with a line that was hot and, "You probably know them." Well, I thought, I'll call back to see what this is all about. Cutting through the small talk I urged him to get to the point, to which he replied "Well, it's 'XYZ Corp.'"

"XYZ Corp." was a line that years earlier had talked to me about my territory and a major account in particular they had tried themselves and through other reps, to sell to. XYZ Corp. hemmed and hawed but finally told me if I could get a P.O. from that account within two months, they'd give me a territory.

You know where this is going. I delivered a Purchase Order within *two weeks* from this "problem account." And they reneged on their word, not giving me any territory at all, *and* not even paying me for the one order I turned into them.

Who needs referrals from scuzzballs? Use your good contacts to full advantage and remember to ask *them* for referrals.

E. Your Résumé

With all these techniques in matching you to vendors for whom you want to sell, you'll need a good résumé. It should look good printed, of course, but it should also be in your hard drive so you can quickly email it to someone who contacts you via phone or email. If you have to fax it (less likely these days) it can also be used that way as well.

Don't waste your money with a professional who writes résumés for job seekers. For one thing, I'm not alone in thinking that 99% of those types of résumés are pure crap. It's good to know my son's Middle School "Career

Investigations" teacher agrees. The majority of "profession-
ally written" résumés are full of platitudinous nonsense, like:

> Motivated Individual seeks dynamic opportunity in
> order to fulfill strategic and tactical synergies and
> achieve pre-ordained capabilities in order to ce-
> ment partnerships in common goals...

And all this for a gal who wants to be a greeting host-
ess in a restaurant or similar job. Who on earth actually
reads these résumés, let alone employs anyone who uses
them? And ever notice they are almost *always* two pages long or more? I've had to employ people before and
have never looked beyond one page, so that one page
better be good.

A local Dallas radio morning crew has even taken to
reading real résumés on air and asking their crew and lis-
teners to guess what kind of job the job seeker is actually
seeking. The answers are not only always wrong—they're
way off! But it makes for hilarious listening.

Reps are fortunate in that they are almost always
"employed" already. If you are starting out, you can mention your prior work history in a bit of detail, but your résumé should almost always follow the formula you see on
the next page.

Keep it limited to one page; don't feel like you have to list
every line you carry, just the best ones and enough to give
the prospective vendor an idea of what you are capable
of. And list the references who'll speak most highly of you.

If you list nothing but fishing reel manufacturers when
you, in fact, also sell lures, line, hip waders, and tackle
boxes, you're missing the point. Those reel manufacturers
may be among the top of the heap in the fishing tackle
business, but it won't convey a sense of how flexible you
are on your résumé.

Sample Résumé

Name
Your Company Name
Address
City, State, Zip Code
Phone and Fax #s
Email address
Website address

Lines carried:
Company A, City/State of location, phone, contact person
Company B, same info, etc.
Anywhere from 6-12 such company listings should be enough

Note: if you want to segregate lines by product types or note what they sell after their names in the listing, that is OK.

Territory Covered:
List states, Countries, etc.

Types of Accounts called on:
Sporting Goods Stores, Health spas, etc., or whatever your account base looks like

Some of your major accounts called on:
XYZ Corp, Genuine Texas Hubcaps, Wal-Mart, and Sears
Note: if you wish to include contact people at your accounts, go ahead, but warn them you are doing so. You must avoid having a vendor attempt to bypass you and sell direct, so make sure it's someone you can trust, and who know you'll use them as a reference.

Other background data:
What experience prior to repping you have, who are your subreps (or just mention you have several in the locations they are based), How long you've been in business, and that you'll provide more references if asked.

Prior experience before you were a rep may be important to establish your credibility in a certain industry. I would leave out schooling unless you served as an intern or got work-study credits with contacts that could boost your image in your chosen field. If you have more than ten years under your belt in a certain field, schooling can be left off your résumé.

Think of what the prospective vendors are looking for and how this résumé will help them. Limit it to one page to make it quick and easy, some names to call in order to check you out, and they may very well know some of those names already so be sure the references you give are going to say positive things about your work. Also make your contact info complete (and current) so that when a vendor decides to use your services he or she can fill out a Rolodex® card, put your email in an email address book, speed dial you on his or her phone, etc.

In my own experience, I've latched onto lines mostly from referrals or just word-of-mouth. My industry is small enough to be that way. In the first few years I actively sought lines similar to the ones I had (and were the types I wanted more of). After a while, my reputation grew to the point that I was getting called far more often than I was doing any calling; in other words, they were seeking *me* out more often than me seeking *them*.

Many of my vendor contacts move from one company to the next and take their preferences (like me) with them, yet when they move on again, I still retain the line(s) they hired me for anyway. How cool is that? Some of my best lines are that way, and yet the contact person who originally brought me those lines may have left the industry entirely.

Compare this aspect of being an indie rep to working for one company as an employee! For example, look at being an assistant coach or coordinator in the NFL, where you may be tied to one particular head coach, and *his* job may only last an average of four years! You can only coach/assistant coach one team at a time, but as a rep there is no limit to the amount of companies you can sell for.

It's important to still attend industry functions like trade shows and stay active in your industry's community. If you want your industry to maintain interest in you, you've got to show continued interest in your industry.

Vendors Who Ask For Your Client List
Under no circumstance should you ever give any vendor, whether prospective or established, your list of accounts, prospects or even leads. We discussed this earlier in this chapter. Your Rolodex® or database list of customers or future customers, is of high value. However well intentioned any vendor may be when making this request, don't do it. The list could fall into the hands of their in-house sales crew, or a competing rep group. If they say they just want to be sure you're not going to call on any of their house accounts (or accounts belonging to another rep) simply state you will back off such accounts anyway—besides you wouldn't get paid for them, right? When they request a list like this, state firmly: "No good independent rep divulges such information." You can also tell them you'd be glad to sell it to them, and give it a price tag equal to several years worth of your income. After all, isn't the work you put into building and maintaining such a client list worth it?

F. A Word To Vendors Who Are Seeking Sales Reps

If you are a vendor searching for an independent rep via an industry guide, website, referral, whatever, please try to do some homework first on what you are offering to the rep.

Many times before you contact the rep, there will be ways you can find out about him or her—like their website—to see if your line and their business are a match. Don't waste their time or yours asking if they can sell wedding dresses when they are athletic apparel reps and don't even sell women's clothes or formal clothes to begin with.

Also, check the market! Just because you, as a vendor, had luck in one or two high-end boutiques in Beverly Hills, that doesn't mean you can count on that success nationwide. I run into this problem when a brand thinks they can sell $50 T-shirts in a market that complains that product half that price is too high. "But they're really great quality shirts." To you, sure they are. The ultimate customer is the one we need to please, though. I thought foreigners were the only people who imagined the entire USA was just like Beverly Hills...

This same type of advice is given by Bob DeMatteis in his book, *From Patent To Profit*. He advises inventors to go out shopping to thoroughly check the existing market to see if there is already something out there that does the thing a proposed invention will do. If there is, how much does it cost, and can your product compare, compete, or beat that price? If there isn't, are there other things out there similar that would wind up costing less or being more user-friendly anyway? This "homework" should be the *second* step you take after dreaming up the invention in the first place, and the homework precedes any further step.

It is no different if you are forming a new company/product looking for reps to sell your line. Conceive your product first, and then check the market to see what you'll be up against. Talk to people who'll be typical customers, either informally or with formal surveys.

It's surprising how many small companies simply don't do this—or at least don't take a big enough survey or market study into account. Many try to adjust their prices, switch their manufacturing sources, and try new markets on the fly. Because of slim profit margins start-ups usually deal with, they often fail.

Patenting or copywriting processes, by the way, should be happening during the "checking" phase. When you decide on a rep to sell your goods, the product should be protected, and you should either have a manufacturer in place or have a handful of strong manufacturing candidates ready to go. It may be helpful to talk to several reps during the survey process to get an idea of what their market can handle as far as product, price, and other factors. Prospective reps will not only give you a good idea of which of them can best sell your stuff, they can provide feedback from a perspective the consumer can't.

As a vendor, once you have done your homework, found a rep or rep group to work with, and have supplied them with the tools they need to get started, remember this: *They are not your employees, so please don't treat them like they are.*

Realize they have other lines they have to work. If they approach an account with your product and the account happens to like something else the rep sells, that's life. You're still probably closer to that account doing business with you than you would have been hiring some kid out of high school to telemarket for you from halfway across the country, aren't you?

Don't call them every day asking them if they have any orders yet. An occasional call or email to see how things are going is fine, but again, they are not your employees and they usually have other things to do. I know of lines that have been dropped by myself and other reps just because the vendor was too meddlesome.

There was a line I worked one time that was owned by a fellow I'll call Leo. He called every Friday afternoon to not only ask how it was going but to ask about each major account he had targeted for us to get his line into. He would also repeat his "pitch" that he wanted *us* to repeat to the accounts in question. If he was wearing reps out with this spiel, imagine how we as reps would wear out our welcome with these accounts! He failed to realize that we had to pitch many other lines to these accounts and that being such a pest would hurt us far more than it would hurt him.

It may not be surprising, either, that Leo was the type who did not do his homework or due diligence on these accounts he wanted us in. His product was, for the most part, totally ill suited (almost to the point of being offensive) to these accounts.

Any decent rep or rep group will put the best foot forward when representing your line, since it is in his best interest to do so. But it is also in their best interest to be truthful to an account. If you have any flaws as a company, be prepared to deal with it. Again, these are not employees that you can have complete control over. Fire any rep for such actions if you must, but if you're teaming up with an independent rep for the advantages they bring, that means you ought to be able to deal with any disadvantages, like a rep telling the truth about your line.

CHAPTER 6

Troubleshooting and Problem Solving

A good sales rep sells solutions. He or she helps a customer not only with the right product to sell, but how to sell it and how to have the whole process go smoothly, even if it means preparing the way before the sale. An inordinate amount of time of my own work is spent troubleshooting and problem solving. Sure, some of this is aggravating. We'll discuss this later in the chapter. But most troubleshooting is challenging and actually fun, particularly when the potential rewards are great.

A. Troubleshooting to Get the Sale

An example of this kind of challenge is when a major account comes to you and announces that it is discontinuing a product line—not so much because the product doesn't sell, but because it may not be the right "fit" anymore with a new store set, planogram, or other guidelines that the account is adapting to its business. This is where you must remember Henry Ford, who said,

"Problems are opportunities in disguise."

I don't think I have to tell you what problems Ford turned opportunities into. Go to the library and look up how he not only transformed industry and manufacturing but the entire world of transportation and life as we know it, with his ability to deliver an automobile to just about anyone who wanted to buy one.

So you tell the account, "If I can fix this for you so that we can return to the sales you had on this product before, or surpass those sales, might you be interested in what we come up with?" Any buyer worth his or her salt would say "Yes."

Remember: a good (or *great*) sales rep sells solutions, not just products.

Next, you call the vendors and tell them what's going on. Any vendors worth *their* salt would analyze the situation and see if they can do things a bit different to get the business back. Sometimes they can, sometimes they can't. But don't give up, and if the vendors *can* do the changes needed, you'll want to involve them personally with the team at your buyer's company to make sure everything gets done right. These jobs are a bit more involved than just a buyer/salesman relationship.

Here's a first-hand example of what we're talking about:

I introduced and sold a line of licensed textile posters (or flags) to a chain of entertainment-related media and gift retailers. For several years, it sold consistently well. The vendor and I worked on a point-of-purchase display flag specifically for this account (although it could work anywhere). The display flag showed some of the best selling titles with a message basically reading, "Buy these here," and was made exactly as the product themselves—same size, shape, material.

This display flag was sent to each store and succeeded more so than simply displaying an actual sample of a real SKU ("stock-keeping-unit") had, probably because displaying an actual SKU would not work if the store happened to run out of that particular SKU and would wind up selling the display sample.

Sales continued to grow for several years...and then...

I noticed the displays were not being shown in stores I visited, and orders were dwindling as well. When I asked the buyer about this, she explained that the display flags were waving back and forth at night when the air conditioning or heat air currents hit them, and this was setting off their motion-detecting security devices. Store managers were being dragged out of bed at 2 a.m. to answer calls from local police, etc.

Further problems for this particular vendor arose when the chain of stores were re-designing their store layout and planogram. Looking at the bare numbers, the flag posters were showing a negative trend, so they decided this product line had to go.

Armed with this news, I got on the phone immediately with the vendor. I asked her to not only come up with sales figures from the time we first started doing business with this account, but to put them on an Excel® spreadsheet and use the graphing function to chart the progress and decline, then to note that the decline came about as the result of taking down the display posters (The chart's peak and then decline occurred exactly when the displays started being dismantled. We weren't making that up!).

The vendor told me, "Wait—we have a whole new display that's slatwall mounted, and it would be perfect for them; we hope it will be ready in a couple months." When I notified the buyer and her team on this, they hesitated, but when we presented them with the chart and graphs of their sales history, we got the message through to them: "You *can* sell this product, and you *have* done so in the past; if we can interest you in a new display that will fit in with your new store set, will you give us another look?"

It helped that the buyer herself admitted to her team that, yes indeed, this product had performed well in the past. So it was not a product issue; it was a merchandising issue, and it so worked out that plans the vendor had for new merchandising and display techniques would work with the new stores' setups.

We did have to go back to the drawing board a few times redesigning the display unit (to be less prone to sticking out in the stores' aisles) and the packaging the product came in (more exposure to the artwork inside the box), but we succeeded in getting our product back into the account and their systems.

Don't take "No" for an answer until you've heard it about a dozen times and the buyer simply stops talking to you about that particular issue. The first step in a major sale is almost always "No." The challenge is finding ways to make it work for the account, to jive with their systems, store layout, whatever it takes.

With many big accounts today (and more so in the future), just having the right product will be secondary to your ability to work within the systems an account has. Their costs are far more than the money they lay out for the stuff they buy and then resell, so you have to be willing to make it easier for them to sell your product to begin with, set up a display in each store (and that usually means free of charge), manage the program, etc. Figuring out ways to do those things, possibly more, will mean you get the sale.

The flag poster example took about nine months from, "We're probably going to stop selling your line," to the eventual Purchase Order for $30,000 that got the product back into the stores. It may have taken many man-hours on the supplier's part (mostly me and the Managing Director of the company involved, plus some of her staff), and some may think, "For a measly $30K order?" No! The point is we installed a system that, with very little tweaking, should be in these stores for years. Now all we have to do is sit back and take the reorders. Orders are fun, but your real money is often in reorders and growth. And this line *grew*.

All of this presumes that the flag poster company is the type of company that could be relied upon to efficiently expedite and deliver orders on a regular basis, and they most certainly are such a company and really always have been. So I have little doubt the future will be any different. All the work we put into this paid off!

That all leads us to the *negative side* of troubleshooting and problem solving. What happens when you have a vendor that has problems delivering the goods?

B. Troubleshooting Faulty Vendors

You may be tempted to take a Vendor into your portfolio that may sell great products, have tons of "hits," happen to be hot at the moment but have a terrible reputation when it comes to competency issues, customer service, supply-side dynamics, and so on.

There are times you are better off avoiding such vendors to begin with, and there are times they fall into your lap. While they enhance your reputation and what you offer your customers, they are, quite frankly, a pain in the neck.

It'll be your call whether you want to:

- Dump such a vendor outright
- Ride them out by writing as little as possible with them (but be *sure* to give all accounts showing interest in them fair warning. "I just want to let you know of all my lines this one has the slowest service, so please be patient with them," is not unfair to anyone, if true).
- Tough it out, take a deep breath, and spend whatever time it takes to get the job done.

In most cases, I'll pick the middle option of riding it out. If I had bad experiences with a vendor and parted company with them, I always pick the first option of dumping them, or more accurately, I don't take them on again the second time. And as for the third option of Toughing It Out, and putting up with whatever shortcomings they had, I've almost always regretted it in hindsight.

Why? Easy: If a vendor loses orders, doesn't check orders after they are pulled by some kid that's brand new, doesn't invoice the product correctly, sends the product to another store in a different state that coincidentally has the same name, doesn't *correct* their mistakes once mistakes are brought to their attention, do you *really* think their bookkeeping will be much better? Which department of their company handles *your* commissions?

My business has such vendors. In thirty or forty years of the licensing end of entertainment and music, the lines that were heavy hitters a mere fifteen years ago are all gone. This is worse than the recording industry...themselves hardly the model to look to on how to run *any* business. But we live in an age where an Enron mess, or a $700 Billion bailout of the financial and auto industries by the Government, are possible. Face it, bad management can happen anywhere, in any industry. (It would be one thing if the Government itself were efficient...)

If you notice one in ten—10%— of your orders are ones you have to constantly go back and resubmit, check on the status, file a claim for misships or shortages, then that is probably too high. Think of the time you spend on such duplication of effort and think of how much better that time can be spent in selling stuff for an efficient company, one that you simply fax or email an order into, in *any* form you wish to use, where they can just key in the SKU number, the account's address (as it appears on YOUR form, not what they guess it to be) and you *never have to worry about that order until the day you get paid commission for it!*

I lost a vendor of the "10%-of-orders-had problems-with-them" sort one time, and bemoaned the fact I could no longer sell apparel for some of the hottest bands in the industry. I knew I had to constantly baby-sit this vendor, calling to track orders, report shortages, placate customers about this particular company, but I figured it was worth the hassle. Boy, was I wrong.

A month after losing this line, to my surprise, I noticed I now had an extra two hours per day (!!!) to sell and concentrate on lines that were not quite as sexy, but they were lines that:

- Delivered to the customer,
- Sent orders with fewer, if any, faults (shortages, damages, misships),
- Paid better commission rates, and
- Paid me on time and more complete (if I wrote an order during a pay period, it was on the commission statement for that period. I did not have to ask it be added to a future statement).

What is two hours a day worth to you? Actually, plenty, as I myself found out!

C. Troubleshooting Dishonest Vendors—the Outright Crooks

What we dealt with in the last section was incompetence. Now we deal with the outright crooks. These are also possible and prevalent in the age of Enron and big government (and all the possible corruption that goes with it) But unlike a company that's cruising along in doofus mode, then maybe lies to get out of it, the Outright Crooks will operate from a pact with Satan to begin with.

What to look for when it comes to these types of vendors:

- Bogus Promotions or other enticements to get the customers to order, then surprise! When the invoice is cut and the customer gets his order, the promotion, sale, discount, etc., is nowhere to be found. When the customer tries to complain about it, they are given some song and dance or simply told "tough luck."
- The "tough luck" approach is also taken when the customer has a legitimate gripe, as in reporting a shortage, misship or inability to fill an important order.
- Promises, promises, promises that are rarely if ever kept. This applies to situations that are easily within the control of the vendor. I'm not talking about "We'll be coming out with product featuring XYZ" vs. "We're in the running to get product featuring XYZ." That's just a white lie—because situations can change in the future and no one can really predict what'll happen. I'm talking about "Your shortage is now credited to your account in our system" and it takes five more orders, and twenty more complaints, to get that credit applied.
- Do they have a high turnover in personnel? Can you find some former employee who's got a head on their shoulders who'll talk to you about them?
- What are other reps saying about them? It's good to have peers that are not necessarily in direct competition with you. If they have experience with the vendor in question, *ask them*!
- What do your customers, or *any* customers, say about them? This is even better than what other reps are saying. Can the vendor in question provide account references? If they hesitate, instead of asking them for "references," ask, "Where can I find your product? I'd like to see it in the field." Then ask the store

buyer the vendor referred to what they think of this vendor.

- Any negative vibes from the last three points should send up red flags.

If you get a contract or other written agreement from vendors up front, that may provide some comfort for some reps in some industries. Frankly, in my experience, the biggest crooks often use contracts. If they give a rep the shaft, what's the rep to do? The rep is in Florida; the vendor in Washington State, so going after them in court may not be worth it.

D. Personality Clashes With Vendors

The great thing about being an independent rep is you pretty much say goodbye to office politics, but personality clashes can and do happen between you and a vendor.

As in office politics, the best thing to do is calling a meeting to clear the air. Avoid a knockdown-drag-out shouting match; a decent vendor will not allow it to get to that level since you and he/she are both independent businessmen/-women. And by all means, *you* should not let it get to that level. If it does, you've lost. Always remember that.

If you and a problem vendor's representative are clashing over certain issues, schedule some kind of meeting with an impartial middle-man both of you can agree on. Do your homework and bring plenty of facts and figures to present your side of the story.

When things had deteriorated between a problem vendor and me years ago, I was asked to attend a meeting with the sales manager and (thankfully) two middlemen: her immediate boss and a regional manager who oversaw my territory.

I was given a sales goal to meet by year's end (this was September) and asked to explain how I was going to meet that goal. Typical BS—sales goal numbers are always a crapshoot. If you come in low, it's supposedly your fault; if too high, they didn't set the bar high enough. I'd rather set an overall goal to keep customers best informed and treat them decently...sales will follow. Besides, who can accurately predict *what* will happen in any market?

I did play along though. I looked at her numbers and then looked at each and every order I had written since Jan. 1st of that year. I also looked at what the commissions amounted to for those orders (they were at a certain percentage level, which easily gave me the invoice totals up to the end of August). I compared the invoice totals with the totals on the original orders...in other words the level of the goods sold by my efforts vs. what they actually shipped. This was all I needed, so I was ready to defend myself.

When we sat down at the trade show where we were meeting, the first question out of the sales manager's mouth was "OK, your sales goal is $XXX,xxx, how do you plan to hit that in the next quarter?"

My reply was, "I honestly don't know, but I will tell you, your boss, and my regional manager here, that we're leaving a lot on the table. You see, I also represent almost all of your competitors. The average fill rate for the industry is about 85% or better; yours is less than 60%. Average turn is two weeks, yours is four weeks. If you can get halfway to the industry average, you'll see your business improve.

"If you'd been halfway toward the industry average since the beginning of the year, the orders I've already written for you *would have reached your yearly goal back in July*."

In other words, I was not the problem. Her boss was very interested in this and treated me quite well after that.

Alas, he bolted the company a few months later and I lost whatever ally I might have had in his position. I parted company with them soon thereafter.

The last I heard, this vendor was barely hanging on, waiting for some more deep pockets to come along and bail them out. Anyway, they are a shell of their former self.

So participate in meetings if you can get them with problem people, but be prepared to discuss facts and figures. Remember, if you get to the point where there's a shouting match, you've lost—or the vendor just wasn't worth keeping anyway. Spend your time and effort with vendors that can deliver their goods and pay you well and in a timely manner.

E. Troubleshooting Problems with Customer Relations

So far in this chapter, we've covered problems with vendors. What if you have problems with customers?

The approaches are different since you want to hold onto customers as long as you gain. They really are your lifeblood.

In most cases, particularly with smaller customers, you can just ignore the problem and treat them as anyone else, grinning and bearing it. These are the customers who fax you orders lacking their name and address (and they never programmed the sender ID line at the top of the page when they bought the machine fifteen years ago).

The small-account problem customers might call orders in using a phone so crappy you couldn't recognize your own spouse or mother if they were on the other end. They leave a message on your machine with that same phone, and don't identify who they are, or what number they are calling from...and caller ID lists the name of a guy who owned the phone prior to them!

You send them catalogs and they never use them. You know the type, they're out there, but realistically they are few and you can deal with them by just smiling and thanking them for their business.

If a customer refuses to work with you and constantly goes behind your back to turn in his orders or complains about you to your vendors, you can try giving them a chance to air their grievances to your face, and that may just turn them around. If you were treated unfairly, I often find this approach does turn them around. Apologize, even if you feel in your heart you did nothing wrong. "I apologize for whatever may have caused this problem, and I would like to correct it if possible," is a good approach.

Some customers whom you've clashed with may require time to get over it. If they prefer another salesman over you, and you know in your heart you're better, let time pass and you'd be surprised how problem customers come back. They may have heard enough about you to pique their curiosity. Or, better yet, your competitor has shown his or her true colors.

Some customers are just plain sticks-in-the-mud anyway and you may be better off cutting them loose. Again, if you are wasting a lot of time on someone that is a problem, you're probably justified to let him or her go in a dignified manner. "I've analyzed the situation here, Joe, and I just don't think I can handle your account anymore. If you wish to work within our systems, please don't hesitate to call us again, we'll be glad to help." Always leave with your dignity intact.

What about problem customers who are major accounts? I'm not talking "we're dropping this line" type situations. I already showed you how to handle that at the beginning of the chapter. I'm talking about personality clashes that escalate to the point where you just can't deal with them anymore. Unfortunately, they can and do happen.

When this has happened, I've been lucky enough to be able to use an associate or subrep that could step in and take my place. It at least kept our presence in the account.

You'll often run into other people in the industry who've had problems with the same problem customer. It's small consolation to learn that dozens of other vendors have seen their business disappear, too, all because of a buyer who's a borderline psycho.

Time was when someone like this would be easily fired, demoted, or moved to another part of the company. But since most companies now have extensive Human Resources departments for better or worse, getting rid of such a personality is not as easy as before. In this respect, dealing with private companies has become like dealing with the Government.

Think twice about going to anyone's superior at a company even if it is stated, printed, policy signed by the CEO. If I had to do so again for any problem employee within a company, I'd report directly to the CEO in person, and I would not name the individual until I was guaranteed in writing that I would not be identified and I would not have to discuss matters face-to-face with that person until given more written guarantee that in no way would this backfire on the sales rep.

I would also find out first if there were any other reps or vendors that have a problem with the individual. This is tricky stuff, so tread carefully. If you have a confidential source within the customer's company then that may help. If you bring up the subject with a friendly competitor, that may also help, but you may have to ask discretely, "how's your business with so-and-so's department?" This is quite a departure from problems you may have with a vendor or smaller account, I realize. But HR departments, I am afraid, have made it this way.

After losing vendors, blown opportunities and other in-come-impairing incidents to such a situation, I'm just glad it was a rarity. Rest assured, if it is happening to you, it is prob-ably happening to others, and the buyer is likely running roughshod over people in their own organization as well. In my case, this was exactly what was happening. So it was just a matter of time until justice finally was served and the buyer quit before being fired. Damage done, it was time for everyone to move forward. Thankfully it was forward.

It's interesting to note that over the years, problems like this with an account or with a vendor (or a combina-tion as we'll see in a minute) all work out, and justice does seem to prevail. One of my counterparts in another part of the country had an account he helped to grow into a large mail-order supplier in his industry. One day, though, the customer happened to call one of the vendors direct to find where an order stood. He should have called the rep, but...

The customer service girl at the vendor tracked down the order's status and a conversation ensued where she disclosed to the account the amount of commission the rep made for orders placed. You don't need to be a ge-nius to know that talking about salary or what someone is paid is bad form in any situation. And besides, it's no-body's business except for the guy getting paid, and the one signing the check.

The customer got all bent out of shape and decided he didn't need to be using this rep anymore—for anything!

Needless to say, the customer service girl lost her job; the vendor was decent enough in that regard. But the account also started falling apart. They weren't buying smart enough after that and apparently internal strife as a result was taking its toll, all because the account could not fathom a rep making a commission—the only form of compensation a rep makes at all!

F. Troubleshooting the Commissions Owed You

A good vendor will pay you:

- Regularly—it may be monthly (most common), it may be quarterly, but it will be on a predictable basis.
- With a detailed but easy-to-read commission statement, all the time. This sounds logical, but if I had a dime for every time I got a lone check in the mail without a statement, I'd have a nice annuity growing somewhere. Statements should include your P.O.number or customer's assigned P.O.number, invoice number, name of account, date, and dollar amount. It should show what commission rate you earned for each order (if you had to discount for a particular order, you'd be at a lesser amount), and total up what you earned on the check. Any more info is really not needed, but any less is really not acceptable. NOTE: a new, and hopefully growing development, is electronic transmission of invoice copies and commission statements, making bookkeeping more "paperless." This helps a great deal and relies less on the postal service for key documents. Direct deposit of commissions is another option that may work for some.
- For the entire pay period the statement indicates, or at least those accounts who are paid up during that period. This means that if they pay you for orders you wrote in October, and it is now January, any and all orders you wrote in October for that vendor are on the statement. By now, all accounts, whether prepay, COD, or Net 30 or Net 60, should have paid the vendor for their goods, and the vendor can now pay your commission. There are more details below on this.
- Without you having to ask for it.

I am always amazed when I find other reps that just get a commission check and don't go through their order logs to make sure each and every order is accounted for. Not only is this irresponsible to your customers (did they even *get* that order you placed?), it is stupid on the rep's part. They can be leaving tons of money on the table.

Not all vendors are crooks, not all vendors are careless. But the same people that go through their bank's checking account statement each month think nothing of forgetting to double-check their commission statement. Maybe I'm wrong—maybe they *do* avoid balancing their checkbook!

Whether you log your orders in your computer or do it longhand, whatever you do, *log them!* At the end of each day, keep a diary of what orders you have written. Note the following:

- Date
- P.O.number—especially if the customer assigns one, but if they don't *you* should have your own system to make it easily recognizable as being yours. I use the date. Other reps I know use some combination of date and initials. Others have a software program that uses a sequential number. Whatever the case, assign a P.O.number and make sure a vendor uses it on all documents, especially the invoice.
- Vendor involved—especially if you are logging all your different orders in same place. You may opt for logging each vendor separately.
- Approximate amount of the order and your rate of commission.
- Leave a blank spot for later, to note the date when you get paid for the order.

I keep two copies of each order filed. One file is all orders by date, so I have files for each month. When

I get paid for these orders, I toss them. At the end of a given period of time, I can check that monthly file (and the log) to see if I have or haven't been paid for those orders.

I keep another copy in a file for each customer, and this file can go back six months to a year, but rarely more than that. When customers need to know, or when you want to know, when the last time was that they ordered a particular line or type of product, you have copies of their orders handy. If they submitted via fax or email, their original is best kept in this file, with the re-write you may have submitted being in the date-oriented file as described in the last paragraph. Whether you do this on paper or in your computer, no matter... but *do* it!

> **The *"Customer File"* Serves An Added Need:** *at the end of every year, I send current customers a holiday card thanking them for their business. If they gave me an order during the calendar year, they are "current" and therefore get a card.*

When you are paid you should also note the date in your log, and you may add check number or other details if needed. At this point, if you notice that some orders were *not* paid for, save them in that date-oriented file and notify the vendor. Those particular orders may very well be from customers who are tardy on their payments. Or the vendor shipped it a little late, or maybe they lost the order or it is waiting for product that has yet to arrive. In all cases, you need to know this, and the vendor needs to know you are looking for it. Once again, I'm surprised how many reps forget to do this. That is like not balancing your checkbook. And you know how that can mess up your bank account!

It's also similar to being on an hourly wage and *not* getting paid for several hours here and there.

> **A Note On Customers Who May Be Tardy On Their Payments:** *this is something you, as a rep, should be aware of, but in many industries it may not be something you should address. A vendor's credit manager or accounts payable director may handle that task, leaving the salesmanship up to you. It is pretty rare for a sales rep to double as a collection agency, but if you are told to do that job, you'll need to be diplomatic about it. You may notice credit managers are very rarely diplomatic, but then, they are not having to step into the shoes of a salesman after they are done collecting past due payments.*

You should have a standard form letter to use in order to check on commissions not paid. Send this letter after you receive any commission check and have updated your records to show what you were and were not paid for. The form can look something like this on the next page:

SAMPLE COMMISSIONS-LATE LETTER

Your Letterhead/Contact Info

Date

Attn: Vendor Accounts Payable Person *(or other respon-sible party handling commissions)*

To Whom It May Concern:

Thanks for your check covering the period up to *(date the statement seems to show latest orders you are paid com-missions for)*. However, there were a few orders from that period that were not on the statement and I want to check on them. They may be unpaid by customer, shipped later, or not shipped at all. Can you please check on this?

Date/PO#	Account Name/Location	Inv.# if known
9753 (9-8)	City Garage and Sweat-shop/Phoenix AZ	735990
9-24	Maniacs Plus/Jackson MS	?
9-30	Genuine Texas Hubcaps/Temple TX	?

Thanks,
Bob Salesrep

Keep these documents on each vendor in your computer's hard drive so you can easily email them. If and when an order gets paid, you simply remove it from this list. If the list starts accumulating month by month you need to really start pestering the party responsible for paying commissions or the head of the company if need be.

I had to drag the owner of a company into a situation like this once. The gal he had handling the overdue commissions just wasn't getting the job done for me and was actually paying me twice on some orders, ignoring the unpaids. I asked her to read the "Unpaid Commissions" document I had prepared (like the example nearby); she just did not understand it. Then I told her to check off each order on the list and pay me for them as she checked them off, "Kind of like balancing your checkbook," I said. She responded, "Huh?" This gal not only did not have a checking account, she didn't even keep her money in a bank! Thankfully the boss saw fit to move her out of accounting. (Who *wouldn't*?)

Some programs such as Excel® can also keep track of paid vs. unpaid commissions. The point is, *do* keep track!

If your list of late commissions clears up with the next month's commission statement, that is a good sign and just indicates that the customers involved may have been a little late paying the vendor. However, don't let accumulation occur and then drag on for more than a couple of months. The vendor could be attributing *your* orders to another rep! They could be simply losing orders or holding them for several months to reach the best level of fill (not a good idea unless the customer asked for this specifically).

These techniques usually get the job done and you'll get the money owed you. But, occasionally, a company that closes in the dead of night and is nowhere to be found from that point on will stiff you. You may want to speak to a lawyer about this if the amount owed you was large enough.

There are also cases where some vendors just have a cash flow problem and they honestly do want to pay you, they just can't. In such cases, I have always found the following technique to work well since it soothes everyone's nerves and, when the vendor gets back to a good cash flow situation, you're going to be the first rep he calls on for help selling something he may have landed that could be really successful for you both.

Here's the technique: Say the vendor owes you $10,000 and there is one of those "Late Commissions List" as we've discussed that is three pages long.

Obviously, you should either stop or curtail any orders you are writing for him immediately until the situation is sufficiently acted upon. This is purely for your own sake, and it keeps the vendor somewhat honest.

Next, ask him, "How much can you afford to pay me monthly to start taking care of these commissions from the last year or more that you owe me?" He's looking at $10,000, but if he seems nervous and can't think of a number, mildly suggest "Can you pay me $100 monthly? $250? $500?" He will usually stop at a certain point, then both of you agree you'll get that amount, or he can pay you for ten, fifteen, twenty of the past-due orders on your Late Commissions List on a monthly basis.

You'll be surprised, and he'll be surprised how easily that $10,000 starts to whittle down. A debt he thought would take five years to pay off gets paid a lot sooner. He will find that, "You know what? Next month I can pay you three times the amount we've been doing; so instead of $250 you'll get $750." He'll start to see the light at the end of the tunnel and will want to finish as soon as he can. Remember, in this scenario, this is an honest individual you're dealing with.

By the way, if you have an honest customer who falls into a similar situation with your vendors, this technique works just as well. Most vendors will accept such a settlement.

It can't be stated enough that you should be on top of these matters. It is your money and livelihood at stake.

This should wrap up most of the issues involving common headaches, pitfalls, or problems you'll have as a rep. Don't let any problems get out of hand or accumulate; you'll lose the respect of your peers (both vendors and customers) and yourself if you let these kinds of things go unsolved. You're on your own and don't have too many people who'll go to bat or cover for you, so tackle these issues head-on.

CHAPTER 7
The Sales Process Itself

While we hope this book is somewhat unique in that it focuses on the subject of independent sales representation, there's no doubt there have been hundreds of books written throughout history telling us various and sundry sales techniques and processes. After my spending years of sifting through several of schools of thought, this chapter will focus on the techniques that will:

- Earn you a decent living
- Keep you from going back to your old line of work with your tail between your legs
- Keep you from selling insurance or real estate because selling the stuff you *wanted* to sell didn't work out
- Keep you your customers—forever—or at least for as long as you want them to be customers, or whenever they go out of business, whichever comes first.

That said, there's no doubt that salesmanship has changed dramatically in the last thirty to forty years or so. A success in sales now, and more so in the future, will have to be more marketing-oriented than a simple sales process.

Think of your own experiences on what gets you to buy anything, especially something that requires a bit more out of your billfold, because those purchases require some thought. Do you buy such an item because it is the only one of its kind out there? Do you buy it on a whim? Do you buy the first one you see (boy do car dealers need to go back to school on this one!)? More and more these days the answer to all of the above is "No."

The availability and amount of virtually all goods and services has grown dramatically in the last forty years. This is good for the consumer; it's forced companies to put out better products at fairer prices if they want to survive. But it has made the job of being a salesman/saleswoman that much harder.

Take entertainment for instance. In 1968, if you wanted to buy music, you bought it either on LP, 8-track, or cassette for the most part (some reel-to-reel tapes were sold, but it was limited). You generally listened to your music on a home stereo, or if taped, in your car or portable tape machine.

Today you have that many options, plus MP3s; and while you can still buy music at a specialty shop for music or at a large discount chain store, you can also buy it online—either from I-tunes or any other such site. Or you can even buy the music from the artists themselves via the web.

You can buy equipment made to listen to music in many more ways today than you could forty years ago, in portable CD players, MP3 players, component home units to add to your system, and all kinds of the same type units for your car. You can even buy music via your cell phone. You can still buy turntables too (those have even morphed into becoming a musical instrument themselves, then made a comeback in their original role along with vinyl in the late 2000s). One company makes a unit for old-timers with a turntable, cassette deck, CD player all in one—and even plays 78s!

As in 1968, you can still go to a specialty shop selling recorded music and/or the hardware to play it on, but you can also find chain stores, discount stores, online retailers, and more that you may buy from. In 1968, the quality of audio equipment sold in chain stores, especially discount stores, was iffy at best; today, the quality is really pretty good wherever you find equipment sold.

All this has had effect on the sales process. There are fewer record labels now, and far fewer salespeople working for them. There are far fewer lines of equipment and salespeople working for those companies as well. Now the buyer, be it a corporate purchasing agent or the consumer himself, has far more power in the sales process.

This is because today the buyer knows more. He used to rely on the salesperson for *all* his information. But the salesperson back in 1968 didn't really give him good info; he usually gave him the *only* info!

Marketing is the process whereby a supplier gives the prospective customer information to the point that the sale is made. So if you are going to be marketing-oriented, as salesmen/saleswomen today and in the future must be, your main job will be marketing.

Again, think about the last big-ticket purchase you made:

- Did you buy it because it was the only one out there?
- Did you buy it on a whim?
- Did you buy it without looking at *any* other options?

Probably not…right?

As a rep, you boil down all sales situations into two categories:

- New customers—where you are basically selling solutions to his problem, need, or desire. Here, you must convince the customer that your product will make him or her more money, bring more traffic, or otherwise enhance and improve his or her situation.

- Existing customers—where you basically continue to do what you did when they were new customers. Once you get a product line into their businesses, you're maintaining it, and the beauty of being an indie rep is that you have the ability to turn those customers on to other new lines and benefit directly as a result.

So your job is to get into the buyer's head. Figure out what is important to him or her, and why your product will suit his or her needs. And then keep giving him or her a lot of useful info, so that, when the time comes, the customer is ready to buy, and *you* are the one he or she will buy from.

You'll find different customers are at different stages of their decision making process—and you'll obviously tailor your approach to fit the stage they are in.

Customers may be completely satisfied with the way things are and have an existing relationship with another line. With these customers, you don't call on them near enough as you would an existing account or even an account that looks like they are about to sign on. Your approach should be real low key and low pressure. You may also address some of the issues from a negative standpoint—what fears they may have about your product. Approach this by showing how your product will overcome those fears.

Some customers may be in the situation where they are starting to look at options. In this situation, your main focus is to sell them on the *idea* of carrying some or maybe just one of your product lines. So your approach is to convince them of the advantages your product line(s) will bring to their businesses. You can also still use the approach here that shows how your product overcomes any fears they may have in relation to carrying your product.

A customer may be in the situation where he or she is pretty convinced that you're right—he or she would benefit by carrying your line(s). Here, your approach should hone in on what lines would be best for him or her or why your lines are superior and better than some of the competing lines out there that you do not carry.

When the customer is pretty much ready to give you the order, you still use the same approach of pitching the advantages of your line over others.

When you look closely at this variation of sales pitches to approach different customers in different phases of the decision-making process, you may notice it is also a slightly different way of handling the dreaded "NO!" or rejection. Just remember: all sales begin with a "NO!"

The way to approach a "NO!" is not to simply walk away and never talk to the customers again, nor is it to give them the same sales pitch over and over again. That's worse than walking away—then that customer is apt to start hating your guts!

Remember how Sam-I-Am changed his sales pitch over and over again to finally win over the Cat-In-The-Hat type character in *Green Eggs and Ham*? Of course, the pitch focused strictly on how or where the prospect would like his green eggs and ham, but you can add other variables like why, what, when, etc. in your pitch. This allows you to have a slightly different approach each time you communicate with the customer or prospect.

The beauty of being a multi-line rep is that you can throw other products or lines into the whole spectrum of sales-pitch/decision-making process and then return to the original line you had in mind later: "Well, thanks for that order of widgets, John...and you know, if you sell these well, you ought to check out Company X's geegaws that I was telling you about before, remember them? I sell those about 50% better than the line of widgets, believe it or not."

After all this, it may happen that he or she turns the order into someone else, especially in cases where you have two independent reps working the same product and line. But most of the time, your customer will reciprocate and give the order to the one who taught him about the product and gave him good, sound, rational reasons to buy it: *you*.

You're the *expert* who's educated him on the whole process. This is the old "you scratch my back" law of reciprocity.

The "do unto others" approach does work, and don't get distressed if the customer does give an order to someone else. Keep at it; he or she will eventually come around! Especially if something goes wrong and you get a call for help. "Well John, I wish I could help you; you didn't give the order to me. It could be hard to solve this problem. Tell you what, I'll see what I can do, but in the future, contact me on *everything,* and maybe we can minimize such incidents."

A. Match the line to the account—where your contacts come in handy.

We've mentioned already that your Rolodex®/contact list is your most important possession. You'll want to keep it growing with new leads/prospects (read: eventual customers) all the time (more on that later).

This is where relationship selling comes in handy. Don't just rely on email blasts or a website; pick up the phone and try to talk to as many of your customers, regularly, as much as you can. Try to visit their stores; even if the store is out of your area, maybe they have a website and a webcam. Check it out.

When you get a new line, think carefully about where it works best. If a particular customer has a store where they are selling stuff like this new line, use that approach. "Joe, I picked up XYZ Co.'s line and I'm sending you a catalog immediately; you can sell this stuff. I know it!"

Maybe an old line that you've had matches an account now where it didn't five years ago. "Joe, you told me you might cut back on your stock of CDs. What do you plan on filling that floor space with? Do you remember ABC Co, that line that sells video game related items? Well, I think your customers are going to be more apt to buy this line and make you money than anything else you can replace CDs with."

Or, "How were your holiday sales figures, Joe? Down again? Say, do you remember that line I sent you a catalog on a few months ago? Check it again and look at the new stuff they have on my website. I have an account a lot like you in another state and he is selling the daylights out of that line. It may not turn your sales completely around, but hey, it's a start, isn't it?"

A retailer would have to be nuts not to start seriously thinking about what you've said because, after all, how many other salesmen are saying those types of things?

Beware of the shotgun approach where you treat every account the same. Email newsletters are fine, but if you can tailor them with a little editing to fit the account, so much the better.

There is software available at www.freetranslation.com that can be added to your Word© or Outlook© programs that will translate your message to any one of several languages. Think of that advantage when dealing with overseas accounts that may very well know English, but how do you think they'll react seeing something in their own language, even if it is a bit flawed? (A computer is doing the work, remember) It is still going to stick in their minds if you've "translated" your message to suit them.

Don't rely on simple email blasts or your website as the only means of communication. Try calling or visiting your accounts personally. It is getting harder to do this, and more retailers are showing less time to spend listening to or getting a visit from a salesman, but it personalizes the pitch and the relationship. It also provides valuable feedback to you, the sales rep.

The action of Sales is like anything else. You should focus on listening more than talking. Some accounts may not give you feedback, but those that do will give you information that could lead to major advantages over your competition.

When it really mattered in the early 90s, one of my lines insisted on us reps giving them feedback from accounts as to what bands were hot at the time and being requested for licensed goods. This was before kids quit caring that much about current music trends and before email had become common, so I used postcards to correspond to the CEO of this particular line. He read them and signed deals on many of my suggestions. Some of these bands stayed with his company for years, and I was able to sell their goods all that time.

You may have some lines in mind that you picked up with only a handful of accounts, or prospects you'd like to add to your customer base. Be careful not to pitch those lines to some account that has absolutely no use for them. If you fall into this practice, the account will react to your communication the way we all react to junk mail or spam.

A worst-case scenario is to pitch a particular item that an account has just flat out said they won't carry. That's their prerogative, and if the item is huge and selling in a thousand other places, it may be understandable if the customer doesn't want it; it'll mean price wars or a lot of overstock when the item fades from popularity as is often the case.

Many in my industry wore out their welcome pushing wrestling T-shirts or other fads in accounts that stated more than once they were not going to get into those specific fads. "No," followed by an explanation usually does mean "No." Saying "OK, but if you change your mind let me know," will not offend any customer.

Remember the story about the trade show my associate and I went to? Giving out catalog packets became easier when we referred to them as "Gift Packs." Make your pitch look like it is directed at that customer and him or her alone. Then let the law of reciprocity kick in. You'll be the one likely to get the orders.

Supposedly, the two most effective words in advertising and marketing are "Free" and "You." While we can only do a limited amount of things in the former category, we can do quite a lot by focusing on using the concept "You" to a prospect.

B. Leads—acting on them and follow-up

It amazes me how many times I hear about potential customers asking for more info and a rep that doesn't get around, or refuses, to act upon it! It is even more amazing that there are companies out there that will get inquiries on their site or at trade shows and then turn these leads over to the rep for that geographic area, and still the reps don't work on them!

Surely you've heard the old adage that, in business, customers are your whole reason for being. Specifically in sales, the only way you grow customers is by leads— whether you scope them out yourself, they come to you, or in the best way possible, someone *hands* them to you.

When you get leads handed to you, the one who hands off has to feel confident you'll do something with them. If you develop a habit of not doing so, guess what? Or rather, I should say, guess *who* will get those leads in the future? Answer: anyone *but* you!

When you have a lead contact you, always be sure to ask, "Where did you hear about me?" This way, if you are advertising or listing yourself, somehow you'll know that way is working, and that if the ad/list agency wants you to continue to advertise/list with them, you'd better renew the ad! If they say they saw your website, ask what search engine they used—Google, Ask.com, Yahoo, etc. The great thing about leads coming to you on their own volition is that they are probably more ripe to buy from you.

Remember the adage most retailers live by (or at least they ought to): 100% of everyone who walks into your store is a potential customer. Think about that. Why else are they in the store? To use the bathroom? OK, OK, maybe they are a salesman or a competitor, but you get the point. "Just looking," means they are a potential customer and someone who asks you, a sales rep, for more info is doing the same kind of thing.

Pay attention also to the way you find leads yourself. Was it an ad in a trade publication, online, or in the *Yellow Pages*? Sometimes, those free weekly newspapers distributed in most major cities can be a great source for certain businesses—specialty retailers, restaurants, and specific service providers. These businesses may be small in size, but there are a lot of them, and they may not be able to advertise like the major retailers who advertise in the big metropolitan dailies.

Be wary of leads lists you buy from companies specializing in sales of such lists. Most I've come across have been terrible—padded with accounts that are out of business or have nothing to do with the industry they are supposed to represent. If you do come across such a list, see if there is a "try it free" option before you buy anything bigger.

Using the *Yellow Pages* or online versions of phone directories is a pretty good way to find leads that are targeted in the specific industry field you are after. Trade papers or other industry-specific publications are another good source of leads; sometimes, these publications sell an industry guide that not only includes the name, address, and phone number, they may also include website and name contacts. These guides are usually nothing more than subscriber lists, but they can be good lead sources.

Cultivating leads and prospects is the main task of marketing and is the best, easiest way you get your business to grow. You should always pay particular attention to this task because you don't know where your existing accounts will be tomorrow. They could be out of business or sold to someone from out of your territory.

When you get a lead,

- **Contact them**. Phoning is best, or visit if you can. (With overseas accounts, you may have to rely on email, but that's understandable.) Talk to them and let them tell you what they need! This is real important, if you want to match your sales pitch to their needs. Once you have *qualified* a lead; that is, once you have determined that they look good to become an eventual customer some day, this turns the lead into a *prospect*.
- **Get their complete contact info**, so you can keep in touch with them, of course. You may ask them what is a good day or time for them so you can keep them up-to-date.
- **Put all prospects on your hopper system schedule**. You should have all your accounts/prospects on a standard rotating schedule so that they always stay informed. This is what's referred to as a Hopper System. Once a month, in most businesses, should be plenty. But your particular business may need to be more,

maybe less. The best way to gauge this is by your business' schedule of new product development and release, or how often your lines release their own corporate newsletter.

- **Stick to the hopper schedule**; some sales "experts" in the past have advised that, if a customer has not bought from you after a month or two drop them and move on. Oh, I guess every product ever made was sold within a month, huh? What an asinine bit of advice! Keep a prospect on your hopper for as long as possible; after all, how much are you spending to call them once a month to just give them a bit of new product info? A few cents? How long is "as long as possible?" My rule of thumb is about six months after you figured they aren't going to buy anything, because they just may surprise you.

This last point is as important as acting on the lead in the first place. So many reps that *do* make those first calls fall flat on their faces by following the advice of that "expert" who told us to abandon any prospect that hasn't bought within a month. They may get the decision-making process started in the prospective customer's mind, then leave him when he's halfway there. Out of sight, out of mind. And if he does finally buy, he may very well do it with a competitor.

Think of your own experience when you were putting a lot of money into a purchase. Didn't you want to think about it? Didn't you want some material to study in addition to the salesman's pitch? Didn't you want to make sure you were spending your money wisely?

People do *not* always buy cheap; they want to buy the best *value*. That's a big difference. And to give them a notion of value, you must keep them informed on a regular basis.

A recent purchase of significant amount I made was a chiropractic care program that I first learned about almost two years prior to me writing the check. I compared doctors, saw the doctor I eventually chose give a presentation of what made her system different and better than her competitors. I even suggested that my wife check this doctor out. When I saw the improvement in my wife, I finally decided my recurring sciatica needed more than spot treatment.

Auto sales and purchases have been affected tremendously by the amount of info you can now get on any car from sources *other* than the salesman. This includes information through the competition, Internet, many more trade mags, etc. The salesman/saleswoman who works in this mold and keeps in touch with a customer (email, regular mail if the customer prefers a low-pressure approach) stands to benefit and get more sales than that plaid-jacketed jerk who figures that any prospect that walks off the lot without buying won't ever come back.

Hopper systems work after the first sale too; you never know when the next sale will take place. The realtor that sold me my home still sends a calendar every holiday season—fifteen years later, after the mortgage has been paid off. When/if I ever sell my house, well, she has a good chance of getting called, because I remain in her hopper.

C. Regular Customer Contact—Personal (The Pitch Itself)

Now that you have your customers on a regularly scheduled hopper system, *what do you tell them when you contact them?* In the last section, we talked about relaying information about your lines to them; that's most of what you need to do to maintain a steady relationship with most accounts. But how do you custom-tailor the message to each individual store?

A sales script, modified each month, is the easiest way to do this. You can do this by writing a basic script out each month to reflect what your companies are doing that's new, exciting, different. Easier is to simply take whatever newsletter you've prepared and highlight the significant passages. You may want to highlight parts in yellow that apply to one type of account and highlight green those parts that are significant to other types of accounts. Then, pin this up in front of you so you can easily spiel off the talking points while you are on the phone.

One customer of mine once asked if I was reading from a script. I told him, well, yes, in a flashcard type way, but so what? I then asked him what the last sales rep he talked to sounded like. His answer was, "You're the only rep who bothers calling me at all anymore, and the ones that used to call me a few years ago just asked me if I needed to buy anything that day."

Use the same "tailored" approach if you personally visit the account. Give them a call in advance and ask, "Is next Tuesday around 2.30 OK, since I'll be in that area?" Leave the customer some literature, catalogs, brochures, etc., and try showing some samples. If you can spare any, give them a sample if that will help them make a decision after you leave. Make the presentation fit the account.

Compare this low-pressure approach with, "I'll be in next Tuesday around 2.30; be ready to write orders." This is like the car salesman who thinks the customer who leaves the lot without buying will never be back. Who wants to buy from such an idiot, anyway?

Not all accounts are ready for an order the day you visit them. They may give you an order from one out of your many lines as an act of courtesy or gratitude for showing up. But if you leave them with tools like print catalogs they can (and will) give you more orders and usually bigger orders, later, when they have had more time to study and better prepare for what they need.

Accounts will likely *not* be ready for an order if you call in advance—they will work on their own time whether alerted to your coming by or not. Retail work is unpredictable-respect this.

It doesn't hurt to mention, after you've shown some samples and given them catalogs, to say, "Well, that's about it, Joe. These catalogs are yours to keep, so if you need anything in the future you can contact me. Was there anything you wanted today while I am here?" What would *your* reaction to this question be? It's pretty certain: In the customer's mind, he or she realizes you are giving a low-pressure way to make a decision on his/her time, on his/her terms. How can that *not* generate a long-term relationship?

Depending on the nature of your industry, you may want to ratchet up or amend contact with your customers seasonally. Holidays or events like back-to-school can be a major portion of your accounts' business, and should be for yours. Always schedule your efforts accordingly.

D. Contact Via Email, Newsletters, Mail, Website, Fax, Phone (Hopper System-How To Deliver The Sales Script)

Email

Email contact is increasingly becoming the best way for us to communicate in all matters, sales included. It's quick, easy, free, and convenient, but can also very be personable. It gives the customer a low-pressure way to receive information. If you can communicate this way and the customer prefers it (some may not—spam issues, reluctance to using computer, etc., are issues), by all means make this a major way to communicate.

One thing about email, though, is that it is not always a two-way communication method. You can send stuff out there, and you're never really sure it is being read even though you may have send a "read receipt" prompt with your message.

Emailing via a group is a convenient way to correspond with many customers that may share characteristics. Let's say you rep several lines that seem to be specifically geared toward carpet stores, when your overall vendor selection can apply to home improvement stores in general. Simply edit your newsletter or message to restrict it to the lines you carry that carpet stores will find of interest, form a group in your email address book for those particular accounts classified as carpet stores, and they get messages that leave out any superfluous material.

Microsoft Outlook® has a "?" help tab that explains very easily how to form groups to send these kinds of emails to.

When signing an email, always have a prepared "signature" that lists all your contact info, much like a letterhead on a piece of your paper stationery. This makes it easier for someone to get back to you if they need to use other means, including mail, phone, etc. Outlook® and other programs have this feature. It can also be modified if you want to announce something specific about yourself in a line or two or if you want to announce that your office may be closed for a few days—whatever. Do you have a motto or logo? Put it here, just as you would on your business card.

Many now use Blackberries® or other hand-held devices for email usage. The great thing about them is that you know your PC or Mac has the same message waiting for you, but on the Blackberry® you can't always open attachments or send them from a file you may have. For this reason, they may not be the optimal sales tool, but they can be great for just staying in touch.

I like a program and service called gotomypc.com that allows you to use webx technology to access your home or office desktop computer (or any one of several you choose, depending on the plan you pay for) from any other computer anywhere—be it your laptop in an airport or your Mother's PC at her house. It may be a little slow, but you can do virtually anything that your home desktop is capable of, including looking up emails from several months ago, sending files from your hard drive, etc. Imagine being able to send a jpeg to a major account that has left you a message asking you to send it again—and all the while you're at a web café in Tahiti—then back out on the beach again in half an hour.

Newsletters

Have a newsletter whatever you do. There are cheap, professional online ways to put out a newsletter like Constant Contact® that even allows you to program when and how often which customers are contacted. Some email broadcasts may backfire on you, though, since major Internet Service Providers may think any message going to over seventy recipients is spam (I believe this is AOL's yardstick), and may prevent it from being sent to the intended recipient, even though the recipient opted in to begin with.

One can very easily construct their own newsletter using all the features Word© provides—color background, numerous font styles, ability to include website links, etc. An example follows next page:

Maybel Goodrep
Finestuff Sales LLC—Monthly Newsletter
345 State St. Ste 4B
Anytown CA 90000
Ph: 800-555-1212 Cell: 213-555-1212
Fax: 888-555-1212
Finestuffsalesllc.com Mabelg@aol.com

MAY 2010—PREPARE FOR MOTHER'S DAY AND GRADUATION!

New Line: Superior Greeting Cards: many of you have asked about this line; well, we've finally got the rights to carry it. More than 1000 styles, each style available either preprinted or blank, for all occasions. Low Minimum: $100, 6 per style. Catalogs soon, but if you want to check them out online go to the link on our site or www. superiorgreetings.com

ACME WRAP—our best line of wrapping paper have a whole new assortment of clown, kitten and puppy artwork, about 24 SKUs in all, by renowned artist Becky Hinkeldorf. Just in time for this month's occasions and July 4th...see our site, or www.acme.com

MODEST GIFTS—new figurines featuring baby animals—American Eagles, Penguins, Porcupines, all limited and collectible, and cute too. www.modgift.com

TOTALLY TAFFETA—party decorations and paper plates, cups, plastic silverware. A HUGE selection for summer cookouts, Memorial Day, July 4th, Labor Day. www.ttaffeta.com

Best Sellers

1. Mother's Day Cards from Superior
2. July 4th items from Totally Taffeta
3. July 4th items from Acme
4. Graduation Mugs, Desk Sets from Modest

Stock these and you can't go wrong!

Reminder Next Month: Annual Sale and Promotion from Wingding Back To School Items! If you need one of their catalogs to prepare contact us now!

This is very simple, and it can be easily changed monthly, weekly, daily, or by the minute. As soon as you learn about something new from any of your lines, update your newsletter on file. If you make notes to yourself and then try to do it later, you may forget and leave off important information. And if you are emailing customers on an on-going hopper system, you want to give them the most up-to-date info as possible. Remember holidays and other seasonal opportunities—and do so well in advance to prepare your accounts properly.

Don't worry about repeating yourself next month with some of the news in the newsletter. It is better to repeat than to forget something. But, be sure to delete any outdated items such as expired promotions or sales contests.

I recommend that a copy of the newsletter is posted each month (or more frequently if desired) to your website. More on the site later.

Mail and Package Carriers

Regular US Mail, Fed Ex, UPS, etc., can be used less frequently but no less effectively than email. But of course, it should be used for more substantial mailings of print catalogs or urgent special needs. I find that regular catalog mailings, about once or twice a year, where you bulk up and send as many as possible, to be very effective and more impressive to the customer than smaller piecemeal catalogs of one or two at a time. An envelope that lands with a thud on the front counter of a store gets attention.

In such a mailing, you should include a cover letter telling the customer what catalogs are complete and which ones are merely supplements to add to catalogs they may have received from you before. Tell the customer which catalogs should be discarded, for example: "This catalog from ABC Corp. is new and complete; please discard any older versions of this company's catalog to ensure you're ordering as accurately as possible." Try to make the cover letter limited to one page and alphabetize the listing of the catalogs being sent to make it easier for the customer to figure out.

I'm finding my mailing and shipping expenses decreasing as email and websites become more useful. However, mail and package delivery can still be expensive. When using mail, use the category "Bound Printed Matter" when sending envelopes/packages containing any catalogs or literature. This category has a rate chart you can download and print on usps.com. The rates change depending on the weight of package and destination. It's a bit complicated, but you will save some money as opposed to sending first class, and the package will travel faster than using bulk mail (you may not get up to the amount of packages to reach that level, anyway).

Media Mail is a category that can be used for CDRoms, DVDs, CDs, tapes, etc. It is lower than first class in many cases and generally the same rate all over the country.

Fed Ex, UPS, DHL, and other package carriers are best used for your major accounts when they need something from you—literature, samples, whatnot. The use of these carriers lends a weight of importance and priority to your correspondence. There are also regional package carriers that do a nice job if you need to send within state or in an adjacent state.

The last twenty years has seen, in the USA at least, many independent mailbox and delivery retail shops pop up across the country. Use them, unless you like waiting at the US Postal Service location's lines. These retailers are entrepreneurs much like you and will be able to find any way that works best for you—USPS, FedEx, UPS, DHL, or even regional carriers you may not know about that are reasonable and efficient.

Websites

It would be hard to believe anyone who thinks they can get by nowadays without a website. I don't care what business you are in—you need one. And they are a valuable tool for an independent rep as a sales tool, a prospecting tool, and a reference tool.

The goal of your site should be mainly to be a conduit of information about all of your lines, and the easiest way to do that is to have one page that not only lists your vendors and gives a brief description of what they sell and do, but provides an easy link to their sites. This way, your customers need only know (and save to their favorites) one URL address: *Yours.*

If you can afford it, you may want to enable your site to have a shopping cart capability. It is more affordable to have an "order" tab that contains a page that a customer can basically write an order via text box that transmits to you via email. Some of the vendor sites you link to may have shopping carts also; if so, see if there is any way to identify you as the rep, because you do want to get credit for any orders sent this way.

Keep your site up and running as much as possible and refer to it often. It is a lot easier to use than fumbling through massive binders when you need to answer a question while on the phone with a customer, for instance. Just as you have it handy for reference, encourage your customers to keep it in their "favorites."

Websites are increasingly important as a prospecting tool. You will find people literally all over the world who may have found your site and want to buy from you. Just as anyone who walks into a retail store is a potential customer, anyone that stumbles onto your site and sends you a message wanting to know more is someone wanting to buy. The trick is to get yourself looked at on search engines before anyone else.

Search Engine Optimization is something you can pay for (about $250 monthly as of this writing, and that is usually for one particular search engine like Google.com), or you can go "organic" or "natural" by having key words and phrases/relevant content in the text on your home page. These key words and phrases should be carefully thought out. What are the "hot buttons" your potential customers are looking for? And what makes you unique, different, or better than your competition? Quantify and qualify things that describe what it is you do. Think of your homepage's message as something like an "elevator script" which you use to describe yourself and your business to someone you just met, but only have about a minute to do so.

Summarize the types of lines you sell and do so in your own "industry jargon," since that is precisely the language a prospect will use when typing in words into the "search" subject bar.

Don't "stuff" every key word you can think of in the home page to the point where the text makes no sense. Some "tricks" like using hidden content where you've typed in the HTML text using clear or white letters, can backfire on you and get you excluded from search results altogether.

Ask whoever is designing your site for you to make sure the main "hot buttons" or key words are HTML-coded so that each page accurately reflects what you're trying to say and what the customer may be looking for. Webmasters may refer to these as "<h1> tags."

If you pride yourself on having vendors who process orders faster and more accurately than some of your competitors, say so on your home page, because that is an issue that will be important to your customers. Leave off any bland "we're faster, we're better" nonsense. Be specific: "We process 98% of our orders within the same day and have a .01% error rate, according to our industry watchdog group." Ask your vendors to look out for this kind of data. It need not be too specific for them to do, but you can usually come up with ballpark figures to toot your own horn, as well as theirs.

Specify the geographic area you cover, and, if you sell overseas, say so. Sometimes the dollar is a real bargain. There are always foreign companies wanting American goods. And they also value American know-how. Just dealing with you is going to be something that may be very beneficial to them, because the tide may reverse in the future and the dollar may increase in value, making their goods more attractive to us here in the USA. These kinds of relationships can last a long time, and what better way to sell than by a website that is open all the time around the world?

Search Engine Optimization is so crucial that you should think of hiring a special consultant for this, or at least spend a good deal of time brainstorming it. Write several scripts and ask valued customers what they think works best.

I was asked for advice several times by a customer who was also a manufacturer of T-shirts and other souvenirs for a major university that is known for having rabid students and even more enthusiastic alumni (those of you in Texas probably know what school I'm referring to, but I will leave it unnamed). He had spent a lot of money on marketing, particularly on his website, but he kept seeing competitors stealing business away from him and could not understand why, particularly when he was an obviously superior company in many respects.

I looked at his website and figured it out immediately. He hinted, but only hinted, at his company's strengths as opposed to his competition. But his home page lacked key words and phrases that someone who was searching for product for the school would use—nicknames, slang, fighting words, characteristics that would put his site right to the top (or at least on the first page) of the major search engines.

Think of a site for the University of Notre Dame that left off the word "Irish" when it came to buying football souvenirs online. That is about what was happening here.

I think my friend had one or two more facelifts of his site before I started to see his showing improve in the search engines. But at what cost?

You really don't need to spend too much as an indie rep to get a good, effective site. Stick to:

- An effective home page with the text containing the key words and phrases your customers will be looking for.
- Another page listing your vendors and what they do, in a few sentences. Include things like minimum order policies, etc. Have the ability to link to the vendors' sites from this page.
- A page for your current newsletter.
- A page listing all your contact info, including those of any associates you have that work with or for you.
- An order tab—this basically captures the customers' shipping address, etc., and then has a box into which they can type an email message. This box can be minimized while they view your various vendors' sites.

I had, and still have, a college student design and maintain a site such as this, and it is not only affordable, it is effective.

We could go on and on about website design, but that's another book. Just stick to the basics of what your work is all about and any competent Webmaster can put it together for you.

Don't get suckered into cool graphics that animate, explode, and take ten minutes or more to load (and which everyone always clicks "skip intro" to get away from). Avoid using Flash for intros or navigation elements. If you use these instead of a well-written home page text, search engines can't detect the important text or links that will drive customers to you. Spend your money wisely; a useful and effective site should not cost you an arm and a leg.

Fax machines

As a sales tool, these are not that effective anymore, since you can usually transmit more legible documents via email. Email also gives you color that faxes never really had a chance to do. As discussed previously in this book, though, they still have their use as a way to have orders sent to you, to transmit sensitive info like credit card numbers, etc. And they are good for things that need to be done quickly but where legibility is not that big an issue. Signing a standard form, for instance, and faxing it, will often suffice until a hard copy can be mailed.

Just make sure they work! Have a separate number designated for the fax and nothing else. Make sure it answers with its tone after four rings or less. Nothing is more infuriating than trying to fax something, and someone picks up the line and says, "hello?" and has no idea how to turn the fax function on.

Phone

Alexander Graham Bell's invention is not going away, friends. You can use your home phone or cell phone, paid for at a rate far cheaper than they were charging twenty years ago. Things like caller ID may prevent you from getting through to your party if you're a sales rep, but the back and forth communication is so valuable it ensures the telephone's place in salesmanship, maybe forever.

> ### Beating Caller ID
> *Have accounts that won't pick up the phone because it's you they see on caller ID and they're busy? Try *67, then dial the number, but don't be too big a pest. The ID will show "Blocked Call". Effective especially when you need to contact them about a shipping problem, payment issue, or other urgent matter.*

Everyone is busier nowadays, true. Buyers working for large corporate accounts have all kinds of screening to prevent them from wasting too much time on the phone— that is understandable. But always try to keep in touch with as many, if not all, your accounts by phone. How else are you going to listen? And listening is one of the lost arts, one of the secret weapons, of a good sales rep.

I've had old friends working at major accounts who may not have been the primary buyers I was dealing with but they gave me valuable info about the direction of the company to help me with those buyers who weren't so communicative.

The network of indie storeowners and managers that I've talked to for years has been real valuable for feedback. These stores are the foot soldiers in any industry.

Just as General Omar Bradley beat General George Patton out for the job of leading the WWII American Forces into Europe on D-day, you will excel if you have a firm knowledge of what these "foot soldiers" are experiencing and saying. Bradley made sure his soldiers had clean socks and warm food. Patton simply wanted to get to Berlin as fast as possible—an admirable goal, but on whose backs? Their commander Eisenhower wisely saw the difference.

I've even downloaded an audio record program for my PC that I can record phone conversations to and save when my customers have a gripe or other dirty laundry to air about some of my accounts. I get their permission, of course. You ought to see the faces of the vendors when I play these back. Many of them may suspect their service is bad, but when they *hear* the frustration in that voice on the phone, there is no substitute (remember the Motorcycle shop that wanted catalogs?).

I get two, three, or four times as many, "hey, do you carry so-and-so or such-and-such?" in a phone conversation as I do in any written correspondence (fax, email, whatever). That's called upsell potential, something retailers and fast food chains would kill for if it were that easy!

I don't use it as much as I see it used overseas, but SMS text messaging I would classify as phone use. For short messages, it seems to have its adherents.

It is getting to the point where the "phone" is far more than that; it's also a camera, message device and music center. Who knows? Sooner or later you may be able to cook dinner with one. For the reason alone that it offers so much potential to communicate in many ways and at an affordable price, I would hesitate to cross it off any list of valuable sales tools.

Yes, there will be some customers who simply won't take your call, but those that do answer are providing you a valuable service far beyond the orders they give you.

Have you noticed that, still—in this day and age of "do not call lists"—many companies either have in-house telemarketing staffs or still hire outside telemarketers to drum up business? These are the cold calls you get at home during dinner or get you out of the shower. Most people *have* signed up for the "do not call list" so these annoying calls are something that was far more common yesterday.

But the fact that companies still do it anyway ought to tell you something. Rather than use their shotgun approach and simply call every number (they used to do it in numerical order, by the way) in an area code, they have fine-tuned their target customers so that they are getting people who have something in common with the company to begin with. In other words, they are doing kind of the same thing *you* are doing (or should be) in a business-to-business relationship: qualifying your customers.

I'm not advocating calling vast lists of numbers at inconvenient times. Your business is such that you're more focused on the type of product you sell and the ideal target customers, so odds are they will at least listen to you the first or second time. Once you have established a relationship with the account, the calls should be a lot easier. So the phone remains a valuable sales tool.

And…I might mention: I still get quite a few orders from guys or gals just reading something off a page of a catalog into the phone or looking around their store through various racks saying they are out of this or that—all while on the phone. So the phone not only plants the seeds, it can still reap the harvest.

CHAPTER 8

Your Small Accounts

Whether you're starting out as a rep or you're a seasoned pro, you may ask yourself, why mess with the small accounts? Depending on what kind of business you are in, these small fry may be "Ma & Pa Retailers" or some sort of distributor selling to the wilds of Alaska and the Yukon.

There are strong reasons why your Rolodex®, portfolio, and customer base should include a healthy dose of small accounts. We're going to explore why in this chapter.

A. They add up!

This should be obvious. For the time spent on them, put it all together and they can contribute to a healthy commission check. You know they'll be around for a while too, and there are always new ones popping up if you're fishing for leads in the proper way (see chapter 7).

Your résumé is going to look good by reflecting the heavy hitters and household names—your big accounts—but do you really want to concentrate *solely* on them? (Warning: see sidebar in Chapter 4 about the Demise of a Major Rep Group). I know the temptation is there—once you can nab a few big accounts and get some programs going with them—your work gets easier. You can take more time off while the reorders come rolling in.

But in today's world, can you guarantee that big account will be there forever? Companies come and go all the time. How many stores in the local mall ten years ago are still around? And the ones that have popped up since then—are they really new or are they companies that gobbled up smaller chains? Are they headquartered in *your* sales territory?

Those that merged with a competitor may happen to be headquartered *way* outside your territory (and could be the account of another existing rep group, anyway).

Big companies change personnel with more frequency nowadays...sometimes just shifting people around from one department to another. Don't ask why, just be prepared for it. Sometimes, as we explored before, you can be selling a huge account for years and then they hire someone you just can't work with.

So these are some of the main reasons why a healthy supply of small accounts is needed by any indie sales rep.

I try to set a goal that my small accounts, in total, add up to 65% or more of my total business. If one small account goes out of business, sad as it may be, you're not hurt. Again, if you're fishing for leads you can replace each loss pretty easily.

If business trends indicate an entire class of small accounts (like retail music/CD stores) are disappearing, you have ample time to start looking, not only for different accounts that can pick up the slack (record companies have found Starbucks to be an alternative retail source to sell music), but you can also start exploring other *products* to sell into new accounts you may not have had access to in the past.

I've known other reps in the past that stuck solely to the big accounts, and when one or two of them went out of business or otherwise disappeared, they were left scrambling and wound up getting a "real job," going back to working for one company, one paycheck. Is this what you want? Not if you got into this line of work to get away from working for someone else.

Even if an account only gives you a few small orders around the holidays every year, they can still be profitable to you. How much does it cost to phone them once a month and spend a few minutes talking to them? Let's say that's around fifty cents in long distance usage—$6 per year.

If you're a road rep and you've driven fifty miles out of your way to visit them, that's a one-hundred-mile round trip off your regular route, maybe $12 in fuel and an extra four hours off of what you would have done on the trip.

You mail them some catalogs once per year at bound printed matter rates, and that may come out to about $3 or so. You can email them too; you spend a minute or less on that once per month—almost nothing.

So let's say you've spent about $25 per year servicing this account. If you work for 10% commission, a measly $300 order will put you in the black for this account. If you're a multi-line rep (the whole point of this book) you can probably get several $300 orders from this account, making it that much more profitable.

I've often found accounts like this appreciate the attention they get from a rep when everyone else ignores them. And you'd be surprised how many friends they may have. Even if they are out of the way, they do go to markets and trade shows; they do strike up friendships with people from all over the country.

Again: They Add Up!

B. Money is immediate/commission rate better

The other advantage in selling to a bunch of small accounts is that, particularly if they are retailers, your overall commission rate is going to be better. They will pay the

wholesale price as stated on company websites, catalogs, line sheets, etc. They know full well they won't get a
"WalMart"-type discount. Your best commission rate possible will be at the small account level.

The money is also immediate. They pay COD, or maybe
even prepay for their orders. Some that are on net terms,
I've found, are usually on time with their payments. This
means when you get a commission check for a certain
month, most of the "Ma & Pa" orders are being paid because the vendor has the money already.

A development that is occurring while this is being written is a trend away from COD orders. I don't know how
this will pan out, but there *is* a corresponding, maybe *more*
than offsetting, increase in the use of credit cards to prepay for orders with small accounts.

Credit card pay is ideal for all parties. To the vendor
it's a prepaid order situation. The credit card company is
insurance enough should the account not be able to pay
for the order. To the account, it's a net 30 situation, since
the credit card company bills them monthly.

I had one account once complain to me that he wanted to be on Net 30 rather than using a card, since the
credit card company charged him usurious interest rates
if not paid in full monthly—well, duh! Needless to say, with
that said we would not consider him for Net 30—for sure
he'd be a deadbeat.

Savvy accounts using credit cards to pay their orders
get all kinds of awards points and frequent flyer mileage
to attend trade shows, or vacations, for instance.

Some say we're addicted to credit cards in this country.
I would agree that on a personal finance level it is alarm-
ing and the financial woes of late 2008 prove this. But for
the small businessman who uses them wisely, they can be
very beneficial and all parties wind up winning. Any small
account that can't find a card isn't looking; all they have

to do is check their junk mail where at least one solicitation a week will come their way.

The trend toward credit card payments for small accounts is good for the rep and the rep's vendors, since they, as I said before, are immediate payments. With CODs, sometimes carriers (UPS, FedEx, etc.) hold onto the cashiers checks or company checks for an extra month or more. (Why is anyone's guess.)

When the small account can get approved for Net 30 status, you as the rep may be called upon to help collect if they go over a few days and it becomes a regular habit. This position you are put in can be difficult, but if you simply indicate the following, you can mitigate the frustration:

- (If they have placed a new order) "Hey, Bob, thanks for your recent order, but we still have an outstanding invoice. If you can get that taken care of, just give me the check number and when you'll mail it, I'll get that order to ship immediately" or
- (If they have *not* placed a new order) "Hey, Bob, XYZ Corp. has some outstanding invoices on you. Can you tell me a check number and when it went out? We've got some pretty big releases coming soon and we want you up to speed...."

It is not unusual for vendors to leave collection entirely up to different personnel than the sales rep in order to maintain the relationship that exists in the sales process and to ensure there is no strain between buyer and salesperson. Always ask the vendor to keep you informed on these matters anyway, since it may alert you to any problems that can spill over to other vendors.

We've mentioned before about small accounts that may run into problems paying their bills. If you act as a moderator and give the accounts a way to work out their payments, when they recover they'll remember you for it; most other reps and vendors won't do this. Just about everyone goes through a period of tight money. Try turning it into a positive situation as best you can, since you're establishing a long-term relationship with the account... that is, if you're doing it right.

Whether you're hands-on or hands-off regarding collection issues, knowing how to deal with payment issues will help your relationships with your small accounts.

C. Feedback/Friendship potential is good

Relationship selling is powerful stuff, and you're going to probably have a better chance of building long-standing relationships with people at smaller accounts than with the people at majors you deal with. Maintaining your accounts should be little more than making, building, and keeping friendships.

Since you're an *independent* rep and you're probably working alone or with very few others, these relationships you develop will reward you on a personal level. In your old "real job" you could gather around the water cooler the morning after a football game or meet at lunch or after work for socializing. But you've left that life, so dealing with your network of small accounts should take the place of that socialization process.

In many industries, the buyers for major accounts are discouraged or even forbidden to develop any kind of relationship with sales personnel. Gifts are the property of the corporation; being treated to lunch is becoming rare. The buyer has to pay his or her own way. So while dealings with them may be cordial, there is definitely an arm's length being extended today with many major account relationships. Also, turnover is a fact of life at majors.

So the smaller accounts are where you can still develop any kind of relationship. Other than a personal level, where does that lead you?

Simply put, a sales rep that loses track of what's happening in the trenches is one that increasingly loses track of what is going on overall. And small account relationships are your avenue to learning that kind of valuable information. Reporters call these kinds of relationships their "go-to men," people they have built up a mutual trust with, so that when something happens they can get a viewpoint, some quotes, maybe even some facts, so that they can write a story.

Often, small accounts are at the forefront of any trends or fads that occur. Look at the fashion industry, for example. Small boutiques are usually way over a fashion trend by the time the major department stores are selling it en masse. Talk to these small accounts and learn from them; big accounts of yours will want to know this stuff because you can be sure *they* aren't talking to the small accounts. They may drop in and pretend they're looking, but the WalMart® buyer hardly has the same relationship with the small retailer you do.

When you can talk to a customer about things like spouses and kids, vacations, current events, or any other subject that doesn't relate to your work, the ability to talk to them about subjects that *do* relate to your work becomes easier.

Here's how it can work:

I'm of the generation where entertainment was dominated by musical acts, and much of the product I sell is still dominated by music licenses dating back to the 60s or earlier, including Elvis posters, Beatles T-shirts, Kiss anything. Some lines I sell are starting to look at video game properties.

My son's generation is dominated by video games—they line up at midnight for new game and hardware releases—not CD releases. My eyes glaze over at video games. I really can't get into them as entertainment. So I have to get feedback from someone. My son...then who else?

Let's start talking to some customers. If they are my age, what do *their* kids play and what games are they looking forward to? If the customers are fans of games themselves, so much the better. Chances are, they may be ripe for any product related to the properties they are enthusiastic for. Take notes—mental or written.

Then start relaying this information to your vendors who are looking for new opportunities. When some deals are made that result in new product relating to the game licenses you've discussed, those customers should be the first ones pitched. And they will probably respond since they feel they had a hand in the whole process, which they did.

D. The Gentleman and the Chorus Girl

There is supposedly a true tale that goes something like this:

At the height of the British Empire, around 1905 or so, a group of somewhat decadent members of the London Ruling Class were drinking, dining, and smoking cigars in a board room with some young women who they weren't exactly married to. One gent asked the chorus girl next to him if she would spend the night with him for □1000 (or some considerable sum back then).

She replied in a Cockney accent "But of course I would, Love."

"Well then," the gent said, "would you do so for five shillings?"

"I should say not!" she said, "What the 'ell do you think I am?"

The gent replied: "We've already established what you *are*, my dear, now we're merely haggling over the price."

This rather crudely brings home the point that whether the account brings you commissions big or small, we've already established what they *are*:

They're *customers!*

Don't dwell on "the price" like the two characters in our story. Make the small accounts worthy to you in ways other than "the price" or dollar value via the relationship and feedback potential they bring.

CHAPTER 9

Large Accounts

We covered small accounts in the last chapter and stressed how they ought to be your bread and butter accounts—the ones to rely on, to pay your living expenses. You need large accounts too—as many as you can get—but certainly they may not amount to as many in numbers as your small accounts.

These large accounts will be the ones that help you sock away savings, put money into investments, and that kind of thing. If handled right, they could be like an annuity—a lot of hard work up front, then just sit back and tweak them now and again, while watching the commissions come forth.

Tiger Woods, at least early in his career, liked to live strictly on his tour earnings. He's put away the endorsement money he gets, into his investments, charitable trusts, and so on. It seems to work well for the greatest sportsman of our age, and it's not a bad example for an independent sales rep to follow, either.

A. Compliance—more important than how good your product is

In today's business world, there are not too many products that sell themselves. It used to be so easy; if you had something buyers wanted, you called them or they called you and a sale was made. It was a seller's market.

The tables have now turned. Look in any supermarket at all the brands of anything—from hair care products, to cereal, to toothpaste. Just look at all the different kinds of Coke or Pepsi, *alone*! And remember back in the early 1970s. Did you see Jicama or Kiwi fruit in the produce section back then? No.

As we've covered already, it's a buyer's world now. What you sell may not be so unique, and even if it is, there are plenty of things out there competing with you so that if buyers pass on you, their not missing much because there are dozens of companies selling stuff similar to yours. There's a lot of money out there, but only so much that people can spend on for beverages, entertainment, recreation, whatever category you want to create. We've already discussed how to communicate best what makes you and/or your lines distinct or better than everything else. Vendors and reps have to make the case for their product versus their nearest competitors, but also for other similar products customers may spend their money on.

There may also be other reps selling the same thing you do. Territorial boundaries used to mean something. They mean a lot less nowadays, thanks to the Internet. The politicians and lobbyists that whine about "free trade" ruining business for various interests are going to be a dying breed; they simply won't be able to stop the free trade the Worldwide Web has opened up. The Internet is making it easier to buy and sell items all over the world for anyone and everyone. Get used to it. You had also better get used to politicians threatening to tax business done on the Internet—this is how far-reaching it's become.

The benefits and values your product and service offers *are* important and you sure need to articulate what those points are. But with the truly big accounts, the major retailers, and corporations, *compliance* may be far more important.

Most, if not all, big accounts have personnel dedicated solely to getting new vendors up and running once a buyer has decided, "OK, I wanna start dealing with these guys." It could be one lady sending out forms and manuals or a complete legal staff.

Compliance manuals are becoming very common. If you as a vendor don't have the patience to look through some of these documents, guess what? Your competition does, and they will. I've seen compliance manuals about twenty pages long in PDF form that can be emailed as an attachment and saved (complete with forms to sign for vendors after they read and agree to their terms). But I've also seen binders two inches thick. One retailer sent one of these babies overnight to one of my vendors, and it took the vendor the better part of two weeks to even start to absorb it all.

But to be honest, as a vendor, it's good to *know* all this stuff up front from a prospective customer. And you accounts out there who may happen to read this, if you don't have a compliance manual, please get one.

In the past, it was not unusual for a customer to charge back a vendor for not doing this or that, when the vendor had no idea it was expected of him or her, or these expectations got lost in all the prior negotiations before the sale was made. This stuff needs to be put down in writing, which will hopefully avoid lawsuits and ill feelings later on. Compliance manuals do this.

Another increasingly common feature in getting compliant with your prospects is the Certificate of Liability Insurance. Vendors must be prepared to submit these with the prospective customer listed as a Certificate holder and as an Additional Insured. This protects an account and vendor from real or imagined lawsuits having to do with the product. If you, the vendor, don't know how to get one of these, ask your insurance company. A good insurer will have one for you within a few hours. If they can't get you one in this amount of time, well, let's just say the world does not lack for insurance salesmen. Fire the one who can't get you a Certificate and get a policy with someone who can. (Honestly, what are you paying premiums for?)

Compliance also comes into the equation with planograms. A Planogram is basically a giant plan/diagram a retail chain uses to determine what product goes where in each store location, or on their website. Not only do you have to prove your product will sell in their stores, but you may have to figure out, "Where does this go, and how?" Is there a product in that category that is not performing and can be booted out so yours can go in its place? Not always.

Even if there *is* space for something in your product's category, will your product fit? Can your product be flexible enough in the way that it is packaged so that it can hang from a slatwall as opposed to being in the nifty counter dump you devised? *Every* vendor wants his product up front on the checkout counter in a nifty dump, so don't limit your merchandising/packaging choices as a vendor or a rep.

Placement on an endcap or near the front checkout area is premium real estate for retailers. You, the vendor, may have to pay for it. They just don't give that space away to anyone, no matter how hot the product is. Even if product is hugely popular at some point, a retail chain will bargain to get a bit more out of the vendor to compensate for product placement. This is commonly referred to as "product placement funds." On a related note, the account may ask vendor to chip in for advertising costs.

The simple fact is this: the huge corporations and big-box retailers did not get that way with a lackadaisical, free-wheeling way of doing things. They have regimented to the point where to simply do their jobs, to comply with government regulations, to compete effectively, and to grow as all companies should, *they have to stick to certain rules and make things go as easily as possible from top to bottom*. And that means *you*, as a supplier, need to be on board with them. They won't be forgiving when little ol' you asks them to make an exception for your own sake. Those bumps in the road cost them time and manpower, and remember: time is money.

If you notice that, once you are on board with a big account and you may not be getting paid on time, this may very well be the reason why, and they may have already spelled this out for you in the compliance manual.

It may very well be true that some accounts grow so big and get so picky about filling out forms and turning their compliance rules into a nightmare that eventually contributes to their demise. India used to be that way; then they decided to get rid of all the bureaucratic red tape and wound up growing the largest middle class in the world.

One recent account I dealt with had more forms for us to fill out than another account I had that was actually a division of the Armed Forces; in other words, the privately held company was more bureaucratic than the Government. In the middle of our negotiations, they streamlined a bit, and lessened their load of compliance forms for us to complete.

But the fact remains. If you want the big accounts' business, get used to compliance issues. And if you are an independent sales rep, it's important that you familiarize yourself with these issues and be very up front about them to your vendor. If you have any doubts the vendor will be able to play ball, this could come back to haunt you later and affect your relationship with the large account.

B. EDI, UPCs, Ethics, Performance Standards

With every new vendor that comes my way, I ask them how compliant they are with dealing with possible major accounts. I ask two things in particular:

"Is your product UPC (bar code) compliant?" and "Are you EDI capable?" If they aren't, or they say "Huh, what's that?" I tell them to go back to school.

Word has it that a retailer will not be able to buy a new cash register in the very near future that doesn't have a scanner to check out goods—or it may have already happened. Retailers have to do inventory more and more nowadays via a bar code scanner. So just how in the world does a manufacturer expect his goods to go anywhere in retail without a bar code? Yet these ostriches persist. "Oh, we'll cross that bridge when we really need it!" they say. I say get a UPC number *now* because they get more expensive every year. The first six digits in a UPC identify your company. The rest identify the particular product. The smaller numbers off to each side are "check digits" that can further identify product should a system be capable of extending an extra digit. Europe, for example, uses thirteen digits—one more than North America—and word is the entire world will go to the thirteen-digit UPC numbers.

Here's a typical barcode; the bottom numbers are the UPC number. Those on the left identify the company making the product; those on right the actual product itself. Top numbers are an ISBN number which is another set of I.D. numbers used by a few industries, publishing being the most common.

Reps: stick with companies that are savvy to this. Vendors: get it done now if you haven't. You may look up someday and find *no* one, not even smaller merchants, will deal with you, even if they want to. When a small chain of boutiques/smoke shops out of Dallas are completely compliant with scanning UPCs, I think it's time to realize the whole world is going that way.

A funny story involving the importance of UPCs and barcodes happened several years ago with a major record label and a three-disc Techno/Dance compilation CD set they released. Some numbskull in their art department decided the cover art would be a close-up of a barcode. The fun began when the CDs got out into discount store chains in the UK...and the items were scanning wrong. Seriously wrong.

It turns out the checkout personnel at the stores were simply waving the front cover of the CD across their scanning devices at the cash register. They have thousands of other items in the stores to ring up, and that's the way it's usually done (the real barcode for this CD was on the back lower corner, but...). Turns out the numbskull in the art department was using a barcode and UPC for *another CD title entirely,* and it was from *a competing label!* To add to the mess, this other CD retailed for a few dollars *less* than this Techno Compilation's advertised price, thus making the retailer lose money *and* reorder the *wrong* title over and over again. Well, the paying customers at least were happy.

Take UPCs and barcodes seriously!

EDI is Electronic Data Interchange. This is something that you see mostly with large retailers and corporations, and it basically means this:

We (the customer/account) send you our orders and pay our bills, and you (the vendor) send invoices and shipping notices (ASNs—Advanced Shipping Notices) by getting your computer system to speak directly to ours.

You don't necessarily need a special computer or equipment to do this, although it may be worth the investment depending on your size and scope. If you or your vendor can't afford to buy one of these yourselves, there are plenty of good outsourcing companies that will do this for you—basically converting such data communication into documents like Microsoft® Excel that are more easily understood. Simple searches on Google, Yahoo, or Ask.com will give you plenty of EDI companies to choose from.

Whichever these two forms of EDI you'll use, you'll be expected to provide:

- Purchase Orders (P.O.s) or capability to print the P.O.s of your account,
- Functional Acknowledgements of receipt of the P.O.s,
- ASNs—Advanced Shipping Notices—which tell the customer your order is on its way on a certain date—and these may also link to labels you'll be required to print and affix to each container or carton in that shipment, and finally,
- Your Invoice for the order.

Ethics have changed and will constantly change. Twenty-five years ago, it wasn't unusual for a salesman to arrive at an account's office, flirt with the receptionist, possibly ask for a date, maybe eventually get married to her. He also routinely took the buyer, and anyone else who wanted to tag along, out to a lunch that lasted a few hours and included drinks.

Conflict-of-interest considerations have made such practices increasingly rare. Also something to consider are things like sexual harassment and other legal matters.

I hear it over and over again how with U.S. companies outsourcing abroad, we're buying more clothing from sweatshops, food from areas that are environmental disasters, etc. These things hopefully make news since they are really the exception rather than the rule. I know from experience that companies doing a lot of manufacturing and purchasing from overseas are making it very plain in their compliance manuals they can and do plan on visiting plants and factories to see for themselves (often with little or no notice) that sweatshop conditions or environmental waste zones are *not* where they are getting their product from.

More prospective accounts are testing the product samples you provide them to be sure they are not going to be stuck with a returns problem from *their* customers. One account I had a few years ago insisted not only on a product sample at the beginning of the product's shelf life, they wanted a new one each time they did a reorder—and it had to be from that particular production run! This is not a bad idea, as the product in this case was a printed apparel item. Who's to say the manufacturer may be producing this item and getting different shirt blanks each time it prints a batch for this account's reorders? The buyers for this retailer wanted to ensure the quality of the product remained at the same level as it was when they first purchased it.

It seemed to work. The vendor in this case washed the product a few times before sending it off to the account, where the account, in turn, washed it about ten times to determine quality.

When it comes to other performance standards, like turnaround time and volume capability, it is always good to tell these accounts the truth as to how much you can produce and how soon. Better yet, *under*-promise and *over*-deliver. The accounts by their own admission may find themselves in a bind and will "need something yesterday." If you can calmly say you think you can get it done in time, and you do, and you can do this when really needed, you're going to earn that customers' respect and keep it.

C. What to Look for in Compliance Manuals and Chargeback Schedules

Those sales reps and vendors new to dealing with big accounts may find their first experience with a compliance manual to be intimidating. It should be, but then again, it shouldn't be. Remember: wouldn't you rather know up front what this customer is all about, what they expect, what they require, what they demand from you in order to do business with them? And don't you want to know how much they will penalize you if you fail to meet their standards? If your answer is no, that you *don't* want to know these things, then you must be a *great* client for a typical divorce lawyer.

Many a good, well-organized corporation has a compliance manual that is either on their website (usually on a separate tab especially for vendors) or in electronic form, which they can send you when you first start conversations with them. Some companies may even have a print version. Either way, it will usually be broken down as follows:

- An Introduction—a summary of what will follow and who in your vendor organization should read it.
- General Terms and Conditions—in dealing with them in a vendor/client relationship.
- Purchase Orders—how they will generate them to you, requirements they demand as to where to ship, order fill, and turn time. Don't expect them to be very forgiving if you fail here, and keep in mind, they will usually ask up front if you *have* the product and when can it ship. Most companies will allow a certain window of time for you to notify them of any problems, especially when it comes to re-orders.
- Their EDI requirements (see above under the topic of EDI and UPCs)
- Packing Instructions—how they want you to pack your product for shipment, labeling the outside of the cartons, etc. Do they want you to pack your goods so that it is easy for them to re-ship to their stores, or do they want it in bulk so they can stock a warehouse or DC (distribution center)? This is also known as Bulk vs. Pre-packing.
- They will want to know case pack vs. inner pack, which means if you pack widgets twelve to a box (inner pack) and then put forty-eight of those boxes in a larger carton to ship in (case pack), they want to know those quantities.
  It may be beneficial as a vendor to be flexible here. Some accounts may want you to drop ship to them with packed quantities of twelve, some with twenty-four, or sixteen. Don't limit yourself to only one quantity; it may cost you the ability to sell the account!

- Shipping Instructions/Routing Guide—do they have preferred carriers they want you to use? Or do they want you to pay for shipping but have requirements of the shipping company you choose? Again, they may want everything to a DC or several DCs, or they may want you to ship to individual stores or locations (drop-shipping).
- Merchandise labeling—they may require your product to be stickered/ticketed with certain information—the UPCs we already discussed, item name and sku number, vendor name, possibly store location code, date, etc. They may want you to make up these stickers. Sometimes they will make them on their own and send them to the vendor to affix while pulling and packing the order. They may want the sticker in a special place on the product—front, back, corner, spine, etc.
- Troubleshooting issues—what to do and who to report to if something looks wrong or goes wrong. They will allow a little leeway here in typical cases. There may be a five-day grace period to report back to the buyer if they gave you a P.O. with a cancellation date of tomorrow, which could be way too soon for your pre-arranged shipping window.
- Chargeback schedules—how much they will deduct from your invoice if you goof up. There may be a table in the back of the compliance manual that looks like the chart below, or they may have a little warning notice at the end of each subject telling how much they will penalize a vendor for not following those guidelines.
- An Appeals Process—who to talk to if you feel you've been unfairly penalized.

Typical Chargeback schedule looks something like this:

INFRACTION	CHARGEBACK PENALTY
Failure to follow packing instructions	5% off invoice; $250 min, $5000max.
Shipping with unsuitable carrier	5% off invoice; $250 min, $5000max.
Shipping to wrong address	5% off invoice+cost of re-shipment
Mis-shipped goods	7% off invoice+ cost to re-ship correct items
Shortage on invoice	Full Credit on shorted items+ $500 processing

Many larger (and some smaller) retailers have packaging and merchandising guidelines they want you, the vendor and sales rep, to be aware of and to follow. If you sell neckties and you want to expand your market, do you honestly think to get into the "non-traditional" accounts you hunger for will sell neckties the same way the "traditional" men's clothiers would? Not always, so be prepared to offer some sort of alternative package option that makes it easier for that gift shop to sell your product.

Many retailers, especially the majors in any category, operate off an Excel® spreadsheet you will fill out for them that allows them to "plug" the data about your product into their system in order to generate orders and reorders, be they EDI or not. It is important to make sure this is done without *any* flaws, faults, oversights, mistakes, or carelessness.

Don't expect them to be very understanding a month into your relationship when orders have started flowing your way and you have to tell the account, "Hey, you know what? We notice you have the wrong price on those purchase orders...heh heh, we're sorry. We gave you the wrong price on our spreadsheet last month." If the *account* genuinely goofed, they will usually change what needs to be changed.

But if it is *your* error, good luck. Pay attention to this detail when you compile data on a spreadsheet! It's *your* money we're eventually talking about! You will either have to swallow hard and sell them at that price, or have them drop the product from their lineup. Neither decision is very attractive, and guess how they will react when you want to sell them something in the future? There is a long line of other vendors out there who *won't* mess things up.

Vendors Who Ship Direct From An Outsourced Manufacturer

If a vendor finds it more convenient to ship an account direct from another place where his goods are manufactured, as opposed to his own facility, be sure compliance issues are made well aware of with the manufacturer too. The account will not accept the excuse that it's "the manufacturer's fault". It's up to the rep and vendor to ensure the manufacturer understands and follows instructions.

D. Payoff Greater, Reorders Automatic

So, with all this detailed *stuff* you have to do to sell big accounts, why bother? You may be making a good living hustling around a wide area to serve and sell independent small accounts; all this compliance and such may be just too much.

The reason why is simple: a bigger payoff.

Not only will the orders be big to begin with, but unlike smaller accounts that may need prodding to get reorders going, the larger accounts almost always have systemized the process of reorders. That's what all the setup info was all about. So it's almost like an annuity that will keep a steady flow of commissionable income coming in to you. From that point, as a rep, you need only keep the account abreast of new product and programs, and when possible, visit some of the account's store locations or website to see that things are going smoothly.

If the account is a retailer with a planogram setup in their stores, getting in on that planogram is a coveted goal and you want to ensure that percentage of floor or wall space remains with you—if not a particular vendor, then at least some of your other vendors.

Once you have teamed up with a vendor to get product into a large account, that vendor also has gone through this educational process, and the next SKUs that go into this account will be easier to work; in many cases, you'll simply complete a required spreadsheet the account has made available to you for such a purpose.

Times are changing, and you should too. Stay informed about what developments are happening with these big accounts. If they are a publicly traded company, read their earnings reports. If not, read trade magazines. By all means *visit their stores* or, if they are not a brick and mortar type of account, do whatever you have to do to see them through one of their customer's eyes—like visit their website. Look for ways you can enhance their business.

E. The Pitch and the P.O.

After taking care of all the red tape and compliance issues above, your actual sales pitch is really not all that different from selling a to a Ma and Pa account. But there will be a few things different about big accounts and the way you pitch them your product or service. Here are some things to keep in mind while you're doing that:

- Competition: small accounts may dread the fact you are dealing with their competitor. On the other hand, big accounts may not even let you get any further than a meeting with them unless you've sold similar accounts to theirs. You may also have to show you've had success with their competitors, because they really don't want to take chances. Pioneers take the first arrows; if they can let someone else take them, they do.
- Buyers must comply too; most buyers have worked hard and may have been with a company for a long time. Being company men/women, they have to get along to get ahead. Much as they may want to do something daring for their company, they will often can't for the same reason we talked about in the previous point: let others take the arrows. So it is easier to comply with what the rest of their company wants to do and stay safe.
- They may not be rich, but they're powerful. Corporate buyers aren't the sadists you may think they are, but they know they have a degree of power and they have to use it. It's their job. It's a known fact most of the buyers at WalMart® make only a fraction of what some of the sales reps who call on them do. Yet look who has the power in that situation. Remember the ethics we talked about above; the days of a buddy system between buyer and salesperson may be something you'll only find with small accounts anymore. The corporate buyers have to project this aura of power and aloofness to do their jobs effectively.

Now comes the time to put together the order. You've followed the guidelines on the account's spreadsheet, checked and double-checked the UPCs, pricing, turn time, what the tags will read when printed, and where to place the tags/stickers on the product.

It may be a good idea to view a blank P.O. from the account and ask which fields you are to supply info on. You know how you go to a doctor for the first time and fill out all that paperwork and the nurse/receptionist has highlighted or checked all the spaces you need to complete? Think in those terms. Your account's spreadsheet may be a standard form, anyway, but if it isn't, this would sure be the way to devise your own spreadsheet for their benefit.

You as the rep may or may not get a copy of the order if using EDI. If the account is not using EDI for your orders, an email attached P.O. is becoming more preferable to a faxed P.O., if no other reason than for legibility.

It's easy to overlook some details on Purchase Orders. If the account has your vendor listed as "ABC Corp." and your vendor's name is "ABC Company Incorporated," call the account on this. They may have another vendor in their system with a name close to yours and guess what will happen when it comes time to be paid? That's right: ABC Corp. of Kokomo will get the payment due to your line, ABC Company Inc. of Denver. Look out for little details.

The P.O. may go direct to the vendor, especially with EDI. If this is the case, try to get a copy or summation of what the order covers. It helps you keep an eye on what is happening with the product (particularly on reorders) and, besides, you'll know about how much you'll be paid for it in a month or two. If the P.O. gets sent direct to you study it for accuracy (remember the example in the last paragraph and, besides, the compliance manual usually begs you to do this for them). You can do this with or without your vendor partner. But don't delay in turning in the order to the vendor as soon as possible—within the day, or better yet, within minutes.

It's surprising how many stories I hear of reps that sit on orders a few days before giving them over to the vendor. In today's "I need it yesterday" world, this is absolutely inexcusable. Even if the order has a ship date of a few weeks down the line, get it in the proper hands immediately. If the account wants an order shipped at a later date, go ahead and send it to the vendor *now*, and make specific instructions to ship at such-and-such a date in the future. If you hold it and wait for such a date, the vendor may have run out of the products being ordered and now has to produce them, adding another two weeks to a P.O. that has a specified ship date and a penalty if you don't meet it. There may also be credit issues, and it's better to solve them in advance than to wait and mess up any chance of getting product shipped in time. Give the vendor the order *now* so they can better prepare if need be.

Tell as many of your vendors as you can about the prize accounts in your area and see if they may perhaps be able to alter their lines a bit to suit those accounts; it may not take much. The more vendors you can get into such an account the better. And by all means, let the buyer or buyers at these accounts know what all you do. You aren't a one-vendor rep, so let them know that, if they don't know already.

There is great comfort in having purchase orders come in for regular reorders from a big account. They are the commissions you can put in the bank and rest easy over. You'll find these big commissions are the reason you got into this business of being an indie rep to begin with. And they are the reason why you should have as many big accounts under your belt as possible.

CHAPTER 10

The Changing World—Sales of the Future

All "how-to" books date themselves even if the author keeps revising and modifying his works to keep up with the times. The purpose of this chapter will be to remind us all of this fact and how to apply the knowledge discussed here of the 2000s to whenever the reader happens to be reading this book.

You might say all books of non-fiction in general date themselves. Adam Smith's *Wealth Of Nations*, which I slogged through one whole summer, gives us a detailed look at (and a defense of) free market capitalism. There's plenty of dated stuff in there that may have applied in the 18th Century, but is no longer either applicable or relevant. Example: Did you know that only one in twenty law school grads back in 1776 actually made a living as a lawyer? Wait a minute, maybe we *should* be reading Smith more closely!

P.J. O'Rourke's book *On The Wealth Of Nations* examines Smith and pokes fun at all the things that no longer apply to today's world. However, basic principles being what they are, *Wealth of Nations* still packs quite a wallop, more than 200 years later. Bits and pieces still pop out at you, and you wish modern politicians and economists would sit down, shut up, and do what Smith tells us to do— far beyond the lawyer bit discussed above.

His observations and advice on taxes alone are worth the effort of sticking with his heavy writing style—a Hemingway he was not. But much of his advice remains timeless and universal.

While this author doesn't quite aspire to greatness, I hope what I've put down here will be of use for years to come. Perhaps in the future, most readers will be able to look between the lines herein and not get too wrapped up in the age this book is written in. Take technology: not too long after this book is published, fax machines may be a total thing of the past. Just remember, though, that there's the principle of enabling yourself, as a rep, to stay in contact with your customers in as many ways as possible. And that principle ought to last forever, as long as there are people who will buy things, companies that sell, and middlemen (and –women) who, with their expertise, can sort things out and make the two meet and strike a deal.

The Internet/Worldwide web is supposed to eliminate the middleman and make information easy to obtain for the buyer and easier to provide for the seller. Don't bank on it. In spite of all the ways we have to communicate nowadays, there are still a lot of people who just flat-out stink at communicating. The method of communication (cell phone, Morse code, smoke signals) is one thing; the how-to communicate (what to say and who to say it to) is another, and that will increasingly be the job of the independent reps of the future. They will have to be a lot more than salespeople. They will have to possess considerable marketing skills and practices, and those principles change very little over the years.

We've been somewhat ruined in the last fifty years since television came along. Television made advertising more simple-minded and turned marketing into some sort of hypnotic entertainment. While many people may recognize brands, they may not know what those brands do. They may not know what makes any brand distinctive or better than its nearest competitor. Companies with huge ad budgets dominated TV advertising with repetitive, entertaining skits that got you to remember the ads, but not really giving the viewer reasons *why* to buy the product.

Smaller companies have grown to admire that style of advertising and marketing the huge companies used on TV (and elsewhere) and think it will work for them. When it doesn't, and they go out of business, they almost *never* blame the message; it was the messenger, or they blame themselves for a product that just wasn't ready for the marketplace. Yet the message was probably at fault.

With the Internet/Worldwide web and its ability to get anyone the ability to sell to everyone and make it a focused effort, tried and true methods of advertising and marketing from pre-TV are coming back. The ability to educate a prospective customer is easier now. And it is easier to target the group of customers who'll give the business that's advertising better results, rather than the shotgun approach TV is so accustomed to using.

Focusing in on what your customers actually want and are looking for, and communicating why your company is the best one to sell that solution, is a far better way to win the customer than skits, slogans, or sales pitches that pummel customers until they finally will start to think about your brand or product. Big companies can afford to pummel; small ones can't and they have to market smarter.

Not only does this show that principles can be classic, whatever era you're in, it also hints that learning more how to *market* your business for the long haul is going to be better for you than being *sales* oriented, which is often a short-term solution.

A. Technology and Trends—Keep Up With Them

Not that one needs to rush out and buy every new gadget, device or software as soon as they come out (they're usually most expensive at that time anyway), but you do need to be able to communicate with your customers and suppliers the way they prefer.

These days, that method is probably email, although cell phones are a close second. One may joke or complain about the shortcomings of either, but putting up with the shortcomings is better than not using these methods at all.

I've had customers tell me they can't stand email and won't give out their address because they wind up getting too much spam. It's ok to fall back on faxes and snail mail for such accounts, although they may miss the color separation and immediacy of a jpeg or PDF attachment.

Such customers are becoming rare. If most accounts gradually want to get everything via their cell phone, then we'll have to adjust to it. That will mean websites that are simpler and can focus on detail that will work with small screens. I've heard that most laptops in Asian countries are the mini variety; the size of what we use as portable DVD players. Since many Asian cities like Seoul and Tokyo are Wi-Fi-ed everywhere, such small laptops become their "everything machine"—Blackberries® are not as common as here. These machines can do it all, but the US isn't ready—yet. This could change.

In spite of the "honeymoon-is-over" reaction to the Apple iPhone® it still shows the movement to one device has potential.

Don't Throw Out Your Old Technology Yet!

So you waited in line for some hot new trendy device, and now you may be suffering through the arrows being shot through your hide like most pioneers, huh? It is important to gradually phase in new technology, and then, when you find after a year or so that you just don't use that old fax machine or scanner anymore because your new copier is so much more efficient, maybe then you can get rid of the old stuff.

Always remember, you're in business. Business is war. Warriors need weapons. Most modern soldiers carry a rifle and a pistol, too, along with some hand-grenades and a knife, to boot. That's about 10,000 years of weaponry on the typical soldier of today. The automatic repeating rifle was supposed to render all that other stuff obsolete, wasn't it?

What does this have to do with technology? Simple:

Don't be so quick to throw out your old technology in favor of the new.

In the early 90s, when setting up my first PC, the installer showed me the fax program and modem that came bundled with my system. He explained, "See, you can now throw out your fax machine."

If I had heeded his advice, I would have added/wasted countless hours:

- *Scanning documents (the first two scanners I had were both time-consuming junk, and the one I have now is slower than a typical fax even though it's top-notch),*
- *Saving the documents (back then, in program formats no one else had or could use when I emailed/faxed them),*
- *Connecting the modem line to my phone wall socket (real fun when you have a bad back) and then,*
- *dialing on my PC.*

> *No thanks, I'm glad I kept the old fax where I could stick a piece of paper in there, dial, and send it in a matter of seconds instead of minutes.*
> *The day may very well come when I no longer need that weapon called the fax machine, but for now, I don't mind having it in my arsenal.*

The topic of cell phones and text messaging came up briefly in a previous chapter. This is one area to keep an eye on. While you may not be able to transmit the volumes of information to an account via text messaging that you do via your website, email, snail-mail and other traditional methods, keep in mind: Text messaging is the number one method most of today's teens prefer to communicate. And they will be business owners or buyers tomorrow.

Granted, your messages will have to be short and the recipient will have to opt in (you won't find everyone wanting your messages, they will have to agree to receive them), but couldn't this be a way to lead your customer to other forms of communication and education about what it is you have to sell?

It's important for a rep to stay savvy with technology; savvy vendors expect it out of their reps or ought to. I give prospective vendors a bit of an acid test. I ask them to check out my website, to look over all my other lines to see if they would be a "good fit." I then ask them to send me an email (I tell them my contact info is on my site) and to send me info about them and their web site. If they can't do this because they don't have a site or they are just technology challenged, I have to wonder how they may handle a situation like an EDI order with a major account.

If someone figures a way to install a chip in my head that will do everything I do now via laptop, email, webx, ability to check my office PC while away from home, phone messages, etc., I'll want in. But it is usually cost effective to wait for the bugs to work themselves out of the new technology and for the price to come down. And, see if customers as well as vendors are jumping on board too. Figure on six months to one year for such a "wait-and-see" period.

We're in a period of history now where technology is changing extremely fast, but other things like fashion or style are not. If you're old enough to remember the 1960s, think back to the start of that decade and the way everything looked and sounded. Automobiles had giant fins on the back fenders, girls had big billowy skirts, guys had short hair. Music was almost as bad as it is now in 2008.

Now, remember how the 60s ended? Cars looked radically different than they did a decade earlier; today's cars look more like the late 60s cars than their early 60s counterparts. By 1970, girls—I mean women (that had changed too)—were often wearing pants (scandalous!) or mini skirts (even more scandalous!). Guys had longer hair—and facial hair. Music in the late 60s has rarely been matched by any period in history; kids today, their parents, even grandparents, still enjoy it. Can you imagine some thirteen-year-old in 1970 listening to the pop standards of forty years earlier? Unbelievable! Particularly to one who was about that age then.

Yet, when it came to hands-on consumer technology, we weren't much different in 1969 as we had been in 1959. There are only two things I can recall where there was a change. Rotary phones evolved into touch-tone, and Black-and-White TV yielded to Color. However, color TV was an industry-imposed delay. NBC/RCA had a system years earlier that other networks refused to accept due to pride. Compare this to today, where technology is a free-for-all...almost *too much* choice and the fear that what you buy will be obsolete in a matter of months.

Fashion and design were far more important back then, and if you were a salesman, you had to adjust. By the end of the 60s, you quit using that greasy-kid-stuff in your hair, you got a wider tie and wider lapels in your suit-if you still had to wear a suit at all. Technologically, though, by 1969, you were still probably calling in your orders via phone, typing them up on the same electric typewriter you might have had for years, or popping them into an envelope and sending them via US Mail—the only way you could have sent them, the same way you did ten years prior.

Thank God that, today, we can pretty much wear the same fashions as we did ten, even twenty years ago, and not get noticed in a negative way; in some cases, the twenty-year-old stuff has already come back, but had you worn it all along, you'd have looked nowhere near the dweeb you would have been in the '60s wearing '50s styles. The subtle differences between today and the 1990s are not enough to stick out like a sore thumb, *but you never know when that will change*. The 2010s, 2020s, or 2050s may wind up being like the 1960s, where technology will rest a bit but where style and fashion will not only change rapidly, they may dictate the way you present yourself. So be prepared whenever you happen to read this.

Cameron Crowe's 2000 film, *Almost Famous*, reminds one of the differences between then and now and how other things remain constant. The film takes place in 1973. It centers around a prodigious teen-aged boy who manages to bluff his way into joining a rock band on tour as a journalist. While he avoids most of the sex, drugs, and rock'n roll going on around him, he does manage to present himself so that he's accepted and fits in, despite his youth and his relatively "straight" appearance.

But what really causes him to win himself over to everyone in the end—his editors at *Rolling Stone*, the groupies, his mother, and the band members as their plane is in trouble—is his basic decency and honesty. In spite of changes in trends, whether techno or fashion, this is something to remember for our craft. In other words, don't give the rest of us sales reps a bad name.

The technology element in *Almost Famous* is not lost either. When William Miller, our teen reporter, has gone past deadline because he can't get the guitarist to sit down for an interview, he is told by the character depicting Ben Fong-Torres (who was one of the original real *Rolling Stone* editors) to get over to the *Daily News* when Miller hits New York and send his article to them via their "mojo." William asks what a "mojo" is. Fong-Torres explains that it's a machine that's "great—it'll take only eighteen minutes per page to send over to us." How far did the fax come and go in a mere thirty years?

B. Marketing vs. Simple Sales

This notion has been touched on before but bears repeating. Simply selling is not going to win much for anyone in the future. It is a buyer's world and will continue to be. You may think you sell something indispensable and that you are indispensable, but as Charles De Gaulle once said,

"Graveyards are filled with indispensable people."

Marketing's job is to build a case for your prospects to buy from you and your customers to *keep* buying from you. It is to facilitate that mindset that wins customers over and enables them to conclude that you're the guy they're going to buy from. So you can see, selling is only the last part of that process. Wouldn't you rather be in more control of the whole process?

We're hoping the whole book has given you an idea of how to market yourself so that you cultivate and get more new business and repeat business. But I've boiled it down to the most important points:

- **Communication**—do it often, and say it in a way that makes it relevant (the new and interesting stuff), attention-getting (intrigue the customer), but not repetitive (quit trying to push crap that's either been turned down or ignored repeatedly).
- **Target Your Customers**—make your presentations fit them by what applies to *their* business, *their* wants and needs, avoiding the same message for everybody.
- **Use Your Vendors' Marketing Materials** whenever you can—Or make up some of your own if possible. Make sure your customers have them. Print, audio, video, on-line information sources like catalogs, brochures, websites, are your substitutes when you and your customers are apart from each other. Use them *always*; they are your "assistants" and you don't even have to worry about them being clothed, fed, or paid. Enhance these materials with new flyers or cover letters spelling out reasons to buy, if the vendor hasn't already done this.
- **Accessibility**—make it easy for someone to get in touch with you. Return calls or answer calls promptly; no one does this much anymore, so imagine how you'll stick out if *you* do. Reply to email. Unless you are on vacation, make your replies within a day or sooner, no more. And for several months leading up to a vacation, let your customers and vendors know you'll be out of touch, and get someone else to fill in for you (preferably a fellow rep or associate) while you're gone.
- **Time**—be patient. Don't give up on sending your message out to anyone unless they either go out of business or flat-out tell you to quit contacting them.

C. Keep Educating Yourself—Increase Your Value—Caddy Vs. "Bag-toter"

"He that's not busy being born is busy dying," Bob Dylan once sang, and it's true. Always improve and re-educate yourself. College night classes are one solution, books are another: read, read, read. Read about your work, other work similar to yours, business books in general. Read the *Wall Street Journal*, other business publications, and trade journals for your industry.

Go to seminars that are both free (usually at trade shows) or those commanding a fee. Meet other people in trade groups; get to know other people in other industries (like at a local Chamber of Commerce), and learn how they handle situations similar to yours. Re-education is often tax deductible, anyway, be they chamber dues (expenses) or tuition at a local college.

If you want customers to keep listening to you, if you want to market yourself effectively, you have to come across as being an expert in your field and having something interesting to say and offer. It isn't just your products you sell that can do that. Customers like salesmen who sell solutions, who can look beyond the sale. Remember that.

If you're product is difficult to display or merchandise in stores, educate yourself on merchandising techniques. Look at other stores and how they do it, then apply it to the retailers you call on. Learn about the fixtures that a retailer may be able to use in his store to sell your stuff. If you're in a business-to-business industrial situation, learn about how your part for industrial equipment relates to everything else in the machinery it is going to be applied to. Get to know some merchants that sell these fixtures or equipment and tell them you'll be possibly referring customers to them. Who knows? They may just return the favor.

If you keep *raising* the value of yourself and your services, you'll get rewarded with what you deserve. If you don't, you'll find yourself in a constant state of *devaluing* the goods you sell, because the only way you will be able to compete is price. And ask any of your vendors what happens to commission percentage at that point. It *doesn't* go up.

You'd think most people would overvalue their worth and think that they are better than they really are, but you'd be surprised that the opposite is often the case. A vendor I had years ago specialized in headwear and other small items with licensed logos on them. Then they dabbled in a few T-shirt licenses, and struck pay dirt with a hot fad in the late 1990s.

They sold a lot of these shirts and, for a year or so, they were my number one line. Then I started hearing complaints from accounts that there were competing stores out there selling these shirts for a retail price equal to their wholesale cost. I found out a distributor was buying shirts in big numbers from my vendor, and selling them to the stores my accounts were complaining about.

I called the vendor and asked him about it. He explained he couldn't turn this distributor down—the distributor was buying in big numbers and paying cash up front for these popular shirts. The margins were very slim, but hey, it was immediate cash.

My opinion was that these shirts were hot, anyway, so why not put some money in the bank with them, instead of working hand over fist to practically give them away? When the fad and craze faded, this company eventually did too. They could've had the cash in the bank to explore new licenses or for new products, but they gave it away. They complained how the competition from some of the big companies with deeper pockets was doing them harm. To make things worse, they stopped using print material to sell and market their line, relying solely on the website to do such tasks, and this was when the Internet was still fairly young; they were ahead of their time but in a way that proved no advantage to them.

A few years after they folded, a new company emerged that was similar in scope to what they did, selling mostly hats and other headgear. This new company gradually dominated their market for this kind of product, and I could not help but feel that, if that first company had had a bit more pride in themselves and insisted on making a profit when they deserved to, they could have at least been a contender for the licensed headgear market.

Oddly, the new company that now dominated the market was nowhere near as good when it came to service as our friends at company #1 who'd abandoned ship. The new company, by the way, was an offshoot of that distributor that talked our friends into selling all those hot, trendy shirts for next to nothing...

Know your value!

When I caddied as a kid, there was a difference my golfer grandfather made between a caddy and a "bag-toter." The "bag-toter" did just that. They toted a bag for eighteen holes, not watching where the shots went, not tending the pin, not raking traps or replacing divots, not giving the driver to the golfer on the tee, not even handing the putter to him when his shot landed safely on the green from 150 yards out. A bag-toter was usually the kid who just showed up at the course occasionally to make a few bucks, or he was the caddymaster's grandson who didn't care whether he did a good job or not; after all, the boss was his grandfather.

A real caddy earned extra money in tips by doing all the aforementioned things and knowing the yardages, the right club selection, the break of the green, the tricks the fairway could play on you. A lot of this took some time over several summers to learn the course inside and out.

Look at yourself as a sales rep. Do you want to just tote a bag or do you want to be the best at what you do? Remember, the companies that use you may just as easily use someone in-house that they already have to answer the phone and take orders—the equivalent of a bag-toter. Even if they get someone in-house who improves themselves to the point that they have superior value, do you think that person is going to want to remain in sales if they stay with that company? That improved employee may just branch out on his or her own and become an independent sales rep—one who's better than the indie reps that are just "bag-toters."

Remember the reps that didn't cut it, that left the business, or otherwise failed that we've discussed throughout this book? I hate to say this, but they were bag-toters. Too tired, too one-dimensional, too shortsighted, too sorry, and too sad. Too bad. Who wants to buy from anyone like that?

If you work as an independent, your only "raise" is going to come by increasing your value. You can keep adding more lines to try to increase your sales volume, but you'll come to a point where a lot of those lines won't get a fair shake from you just because no one has that kind of time to listen to you pitching all of it. You may even have to voluntarily cut some lines loose.

Always strive to be the expert to trust in your field. Your vendors expect it, your customers will admire it, and they will reward you for it with their business.

D. What's more important—your portfolio of companies or your account base?

Your account base is far more important. Yes, you do need a portfolio of companies to sell for, but over the long haul, your account base and your ability to add and attract more customers will be what keeps you in business.

The evolution of companies is always fascinating—Nokia, the world's leading cell phone manufacturer, at one time made toilet paper and other paper products. You don't have to be a huge corporation to transform in such a manner, however. While corporations usually buy and sell divisions and gobble up other companies to do this, you don't have to, to evolve and change as a small business specializing in sales representation.

The main reason companies grow by acquisition and expansion is usually to gain new customers, in other words, market share. When you see one company take over another, and they both happen to have stores in malls or shopping centers, you'll notice the company doing the purchasing usually winds up closing the "old" chain's stores if they happen to have been in the same mall or shopping center location. But there are other locations the purchased company has that the purchasing company wants. About six months later, the "old" chain starts to change their signage to the "new" owner's name.

All this is to slowly win over that customer base the old locations had. A good example is Macy's® taking over all of the former May corporate stores that were regional in scope—so your Hecht's in the Mid-Atlantic, your Foley's in the Southwest, your Jones Stores in the Midwest, gradually all became Macy's®. Macy's® may have had only a few stores in those markets prior to that. Now they're all over the place.

Is *what* these stores sell important? Certainly, but they can always find new sources of product. What is more important is their customer base.

That should tell you something about your business too.

Always remember to work leads, win them over (turn them into prospects/customers), and get them to buy more from you (if you sold them one of your lines, now try to sell them more of your lines) and more often (again, via more of your lines). Your ability to do this is the heart of your success as an independent, multi-line sales rep. You'll notice those are the elements to any successful marketing plan, too.

E. Keep Making it Fun...and Interesting

Hopefully, with all this keeping up with technology and reeducating yourself, you will continue to find being an independent sales rep is fun, interesting, and rewarding, both monetarily and beyond.

And that's the whole point, isn't it? When you work on your own, you don't care about office hassles or inequities the way you would have working for someone else. You may put in the hours, but where would you rather do that, in your home office or at a retail location during the holidays?

You might be thinking about becoming an independent sales rep, and hopefully this book has given you a good look at what to expect and made you eager to get started. Or you may already be one and wanted the book to give you a point of view you may not have had before. Either way, keep your eyes on making your work fun, interesting, *and* rewarding. There are few vocations out there that can consistently do all that as much as being an independent sales rep.

SOURCES/BIBLIOGRAPHY

There are tons of books out there on the sales process itself, and most of the classic authors like Zig Ziglar, Dale Carnegie, Napoleon Hill, Tom Peters et al, are all worth reading at least once or twice. What follows are some lesser-known volumes that have helped me out over the years.

Managing (Paperback) by Harold Geneen—long out of print, expen$ive, but well worth hunting down. Geneen was the CEO of ITT and a legendary American business mind. This is the book that cemented my own personal philosophy to never again lend out books. I lent this one out and never saw it again. It's been more than twenty-five years since I read it, but it still remains firm in memory. The best advice Geneen gives for sales reps is this: Know when to shut up. If you've made the sale, pack up, say thank you, and get the wheels rolling on the supply end.

Monopolize Your Marketplace by Rich Harshaw. There are also audio versions of this in both two-disc and ten-disc (!) configurations. Everything you've learned about marketing is wrong, and he'll tell you why. And he's absolutely right on every count. I've had a real education from Rich's system and, hopefully, it shows in my book; you may recognize some of his theories in these very pages.

The Long Tail by Chris Anderson, uses the music industry as a test case on how to adapt to business of the future: "selling less of more." This and *Monopolize Your Marketplace* are good survival guides for the years to come. I would also recommend highly the monthly magazine **Wired** that Anderson publishes.

Socratic Selling by Kevin Daley, could also be called "Emphatic Selling"—how to get the customer's point of view, to get them to tell you what they really need; then it's up to you to fulfill it. Again, know when to shut up—important stuff.

Green Eggs and Ham by Dr. Seuss—don't laugh. This ought to be on the shelf of any businessman's library. And it will tell anyone about the truth behind sales and marketing better than Sun Tzu or Clausewitz's war books, which no one really reads anyway.

Websites and other Tools

Manufacturer's Representatives Profile—(M.R.P.). This is a survey you fill out yearly as a rep, free of charge, and it gets published in a guide that vendors can purchase. The company is called Gift Marketing and Promotions, ph: 916-784-2300, address: 2150A Douglas Blvd, Ste 210, Roseville CA 95661. They cover a broad spread of types of products and industries that could fall into "Gifts."

Gotsales.com is the same kind of service as the M.R.P., but online. Covers many industries. Go to www.gotsales.com

National Register Of Independent Sales Reps is a massive guide, but geared to the apparel industry. Like the M.R.P., it costs a rep nothing to be listed. Vendors buying the book pay a hefty price, about $170. See: http://www.thenationalregister.com/book_is.html

Rephunter.net—another one that covers many industries—www.rephunter.net

As a matter of fact, just do a search for "Independent Sales Reps" and you'd be surprised how much you find that will link you to vendors looking for reps, or vice versa.

EDI and UPC information is very easy to find online. There are plenty of companies offering EDI services, since even the biggest vendors don't want to invest in an EDI apparatus that could become obsolete quickly, and many accounts deal regularly with these outsourced services and can recommend some of the best. Note too that there are companies that can let you "borrow" UPC codes—the first six digits—if your vendor doesn't have an identifying code. You can find these online.

PDF. PDF writing programs can be found free online and are valuable to a rep. I use one called Primo PDF® that basically acts like a new printer you've installed. Find an image, like a Jpeg, that you want to convert to PDF. Act like you're going to print, and among the different printer options you'll get will be "Primo PDF." Click "Print." Instead of actually printing, you will get an option pop up asking you where you wish to save this image in PDF form. Save it to your preferred file. PDFs are much less memory heavy than other images and easier to email as attachments.

Translating Software. There are quite a few translating services online that are free or available in more advanced forms for a small fee. http://www.freetranslation.com/ is one of the better ones. If you want to expand overseas, having something like this is a good idea. Not only can you send something to a customer in his own language, you can encourage him to speak his own language to you, and you can do this all this through email. Granted, there are some oddities that crop up, as when you tell them about something new and it's translated to something like, "I'd like to show you your Grandparent's dungeon," but they are better than digging through a bunch of dictionaries trying to get the phrases correct.

Audio Recording Programs. There are some of these available online for a reasonable price. Since most PCs have a microphone anyway, you might want to take advantage of it. Depending on the state you're in (check local laws), you can record conversations, conference calls, etc., and save them to your hard drive. I've used one called Audio Record Wizard, but there are more.

Efax.com. For a reasonable fee, they give you a new fax number and all your faxes come to you as PDFs in your email. You can do without a fax this way if you wish; simply telling people your fax number is the one Efax has assigned, or you can call forward your existing machine to the new number.

Gotomypc.com and Gotomeeting.com. The first allows you to access your home computer via any other computer anywhere in the world. This is great if you want to keep all your files and emails in one place and Blackberry®-type devices aren't able to open all the attachments you'd like. Gotomeeting allows you to conduct conference calls and have everyone look in at your computer's desktop, slide show displays, what have you.

FreeConference.com has numbers to call and access codes should you want to host a conference call.

Survey Monkey® allows you to design and conduct free surveys if using ten questions or less (there is a small charge levied on more than ten questions). Not only that, with the results that you collect, you can then make pie charts or other graphs. These are helpful in reports to vendors, acquiring ammunition/evidence to support a cause you're pursuing, whatever. See www.surveymonkey.com.

Free Images/Stock Photos there are plenty of websites that offer images for free or for small fee. You can use these for your own marketing material or for eye-catching brochures, website images, etc. I've used dreamstime.com but there are many more.

Constant Contact is the best known of the online newsletter design services. If you need help coming up with a powerful newsletter that will go out to your hopper system contacts, this is a good one. You can also be creative with your own newsletter if you know how to use Word a bit more than just typing words, then using Outlook's group mailing options. It's good to have a newsletter anyway, and Constant Contact is at least a good place to start.

Trade Shows Are you looking for a good trade show for your industry or an industry you want to crack? Try visiting http://www.tsnn.com/ to get an idea of trade shows for the USA, or http://www.biztradeshows.com/trade-shows-by-industry.html for a more worldwide view. There are other sites to do this, but it's valuable in that they can categorize by industry.

SELECTED GLOSSARY

Account—a customer, someone you sell to or have sold to, distinguished from a lead or prospect.

Barcode—the black and white bars and lines located somewhere on a product that identify it via a scanning device. Used with UPCs in computerized inventory control and data systems (see UPC).

Case Pack—how product is packed in a large carton for shipping. A case pack is usually made up of multiple inner packs.

Chargeback—a deduction an account's bookkeeper takes off of an invoice when it comes time to pay. They do this because of a shortage, misship or failure to comply with the instructions on a purchase order.

COD—collect on delivery. Usually done with small accounts; they pay a check to the UPS or Fed Ex driver, and that money eventually gets to the vendor. This usually incurs a fee. COD cash is no longer done; it is done now by cashier check/money order or by company check if the account has passed a reference check with their bank.

Commission—a percentage of an invoice total that an independent sales rep receives as pay for his/her services.

Compliance Manual—a book or online document an account gives to a vendor that basically says, "If you want to do business with us, here is how we do it. Please comply with these requirements or we will not be able to buy anything from you." It will cover everything from purchasing product, advertising it, shipping it, how it's made, where it's made, everything that matters to the account. Chargebacks (see above) are one penalty for not complying with the manual. Loss of the account is the ultimate penalty.

Customer—an account. A retailer or distributor or anyone who buys product from you and your vendor. Distinguished from lead or prospect.

Distribution Center (DC)—a warehouse, whether for account or for vendor.

Drop ship—an arrangement where a chain of stores orders from a vendor and wants the order to be broken up into small shipments sent to the individual stores. Sometimes an account asks the vendor to pay the freight on this; sometimes they pay the freight. Minimums may have to be met per location. But it saves the account time in getting the product into their stores, rather than routing through a Distribution Center, breaking down the order, and re-shipping.

EDI-electronic data interchange. A system where the vendor company's IT department and computer systems basically talk directly with the account's systems. An account places P.O.s (purchase orders) this way, and the Vendor acknowledges, invoices, and gives shipping info back. This system makes UPCs crucial to product setup in an account's system.

Hopper System—the mechanism put in place to keep customers and prospects informed on a systemized, regular basis. It can be via phone, email, fax, regular mail, personal visits, whatever it takes.

Independent Sales Rep—a self-employed individual who helps more than one company, usually in the same basic industry, sell their goods to accounts he/she has a relationship with or has targeted as leads and prospects.

They work on a commission basis. Known throughout this book as an "indie" or "rep."

Indie—see Independent Sales Rep

Inner Pack—how product may be packed in smaller cartons for shipping. Generally, inner packs get inserted into case packs (see Case Pack).

Invoice—a document that shows what has shipped by a vendor, based on a purchase order placed by the customer. It will usually have wholesale pricing indicated on it, and it is this document that the account bases payment to a vendor on.

IT—Information Technology. The department of a company that works on computers and makes sure that they are all up to speed is the IT Department. Example: "Well, Mr. Customer, I'll get our IT guys to talk to your IT guys, and we'll get this EDI problem fixed."

Lead—potential prospect, eventual customer. Leads have not been talked to yet; they are just names you may have found in the *Yellow Pages* or some other list of businesses that may be the type who'll buy from you. Once you've talked to them and determined if they are still in business, indeed *in* your actual business, and possibly interested, they become prospects until they actually buy. At that point, they are customers or accounts.

LLC—Limited Liability Company, or Limited Liability Corporation. Like a major corporation, in that it stands separate from you, personally. When someone wants to sue you in a business matter, they sue the LLC or Corporation instead of going after your own personal assets. LLCs (as opposed to major corporations) make more sense for most reps and small rep groups.

Marketing—the process where a vendor facilitates the thought-process and decision-making of a customer, prospect, or lead so that when the time comes to buy, that customer or prospect chooses that vendor. "Sales" is the end result of successful marketing. Think of a vendor being a farmer. Plowing fields, fertilizing, planting, weeding, getting rid of bugs, are the marketing. Harvesting and bringing to market is the sale.

Net Terms—payment of an invoice within a specified period of time. For example, Net 30 means payment 30 days after invoice date or receipt of order, depending on agreement between vendor and account.

Packing Slip—document inside or accompanying a shipment that inventories what items are in that shipment. As opposed to invoice (which it closely resembles), cost prices of the product are usually left off. The receiver of the goods usually matches order to the packing slip, and sends it to the bookkeeper or accounts payable person, who matches packing slip to invoice, and pays invoice based on that matching of the two documents.

Planogram—a plan/diagram (hence the name) that basically maps out what is carried in a retail store or chain of stores. This allows for easy standardization of all store locations, making the stores' inventories easier to manage.

P.O.-Purchase Order. A document of an account (of any size) gives to a rep/vendor indicating what it would like to order, how many, at what cost, etc., should also include any special instructions ("Please ship by April 30th," etc.) that may apply. *This is your entire reason for being! Treat every purchase order like it was gold!*

Preferred Carrier—account may have special arrangements/discounts with package services like UPS or Fed Ex, or truck lines like Yellow Freight, J.B. Hunt, National Freight, whomever. Unless the vendor pays freight on all shipments, the account instructs the vendor to use their preferred carriers.

Product Placement Funds—how much money an account charges back to a vendor in order for the vendor's privileged placement in the account's stores. These are highly visible, high-traffic areas. It is also a way an account makes back a little bit of profit margin that is lost by discounting such high-profile product.

Prospect—a potential customer, or a lead that has been checked out, talked to, and looks like they may eventually become a customer.

Relationship Selling—using a long-standing acquaintance, trust, or knowledge between buyer and seller in order to maintain an account. Most Independent Sales Reps use this method.

Rep—short for "representative"(see Independent Sales Rep).

Rep Group—an association of independent reps. One main or master rep, with a direct relationship to the vendors, has several subreps working with him or her to whom he or she pays a cut of commission.

Routing Guide—part of a compliance manual that indicates preferred carriers and shipping instructions.

Sale—a transaction whereby an account says, "Send me this and I will pay you for it." A sale is the end result of marketing. Independent Sales Reps earn commissions based on sales they generate.

Sales Script—a short standardized message one uses multiple times in order to transmit information to leads, prospects, customers. It can/should be modified to suit particular customers.

SKU-stock keeping unit. A particular item that is carried for sale in retail or wholesale situations. A UPC code designates and identifies a SKU. If you have fourteen different brands, makes, and designs of toothbrushes in your store, you have fourteen SKUs of toothbrushes. If you have five pieces of one brand, make, design of a toothbrush, however, you have only one SKU, not five.

Stickering—placing an adhesive label on a product that contains information important to the account or customer. Similar to ticketing.

Subrep—someone who works under another master rep who, in turn, has a direct relationship with a vendor. The master rep hires the subrep and pays him for his work based on what the vendor has already paid the master rep. Rep Groups will have one master rep and any number of subreps.

Ticketing—attaching a tag or sticker to product that contains information important to the account or customer. Similar to stickering.

UPC—Universal Product Code—the barcode and accompanying identifying numerals. Every product in the world using UPC numbers has a unique number and barcode to help identify it in computer systems when using sales data. Whether the numbers are physically typed in or a scanner reads the black and white bars, the item can be identified and tracked. The first six digits identify the company who made or wholesaled the item. The remaining identify the product sku number and other characteristics like size, color, etc.

Vendor—a company that sells some product or service. Independent Sales Reps work with, and are paid commission by, vendors.

AUTHOR BIOGRAPHY

William B. Cornell has been successful as an independent sales rep/consultant for more than twenty years, handling dozens of lines in more than ten states and worldwide to as many as 300+ customers. He's represented lines ranging from recorded music and video to licensed apparel and print goods, plus other entertainment related products.

Prior to his sales career, he worked in purchasing, retail, and warehousing in the record industry and as a sound technician/stage hand/roadie for acts ranging from the Rolling Stones, Willie Nelson, Emmylou Harris, Yes, Emerson Lake & Palmer, Rush, Styx, Kenny Rogers, Crystal Gayle, Buck Owens, Merle Haggard, and more.

He lives with his wife and two children in Dallas TX.

Mr. Cornell has written articles for the publications *Billboard*, *The Licensing Book*, and *Reason*. This is his first book.

If you'd like to learn more and contact him, please visit www.amvsales.com.

INDEX

Bookkeeping 99–104
Bradley, Gen. Omar (vs. Patton) 132
Budgeting 58–62

Cameras 61
Cars, Autos (for use as a rep) 58
Case Pack/Inner Pack 154, 185, 187
CD-Rom Catalogs 40
Chargebacks 153–156, 185
COD Payments 138
Commissions
    Getting Paid 99
Compliance, with Large Accounts 144–149
    Manuals 153–156,185
Computers and related equipment 58–59
Copy Machines 59
Credit Card payments 138–139
Crowe, Cameron (*Almost Famous*) 169
Customers/accounts
    Troublesome 95–98
    Matching product/vendor to, 112
    Feedback from 113, 132–133, 140

Directories & Guides 70, 180
Drop ship 155, 186

EDI 149, 186
Email 24, 121
Entrepreneurial Skills 41
Ethics 152, 170
Expenses
    Startup 58–62
    Ongoing Monthly 63–64

FAX Machines 60, 131
Ford, Henry 85

Green Eggs And Ham (Seuss) 46, 180
Guides & Directories 70, 180

Hopper System 117, 121, 186

Independent Insurance Agents 11

Independent Sales Reps
    Why companies use 14
    Why customers use 16
    Reasons why to become 16–17
    Characteristics/traits 18, 41–49
    Tools needed for 50–67
Incorporating 66
Information
    Keeping Informed 23–24

Leads 115–118, 187
    Turning into Prospects, 119–120
Legal Support 66
L.L.Bean® 39
LLC (Limited Liability Company) 66, 187

Mail, Package Delivery 125–126

Marketing 10
  Defined 46–47
  Explained 109–111
  History 163, 170
Marketing Material, print 24, 34–40
Matching Product to customer 112
Matching Vendor and Rep 68
Matteis, Bob (*From Patent To Profit*) 82

Newsletters 123–125, 182
Net 30/Net payments 138, 188

Office
Setup/layout 43
Locations 52
Microsoft® Office (program) 58
Outside Help (taxes, legal) 65–67

Persistence 45–46
Phones, Cell Phones 60–61, 131–134
Placement Funds, or Product Placement Funds 147, 188
Planograms 147, 188
Preferred Carriers 155, 188
Purchase Orders 160, 188

Re-Education 172–173
Referrals 74–75
Relationship Selling Small Accounts 140
Résumés 77–80
Retail Systems 87, 144–149

Sales/Selling, History of 13, 107, 163–164
Sales Pitch
  Variety of 45–49
  Flexibility 45–49

Sales scripts 120, 189
Samples 24, 32–34, 44
Selling Solutions 85
Seuss, Dr. 46, 180
Subreps 190
    Being one 53
    Hiring one 54
    Support Staff 56

Tax Preparation 65
Ticketing/Stickering 155, 190
Time Management 43–45
Trade Shows 27, 69–70, 183

UPC and barcodes 149–150, 190

Value of Yourself 172
Vendors
    Misships/mistakes 27–30
    Who are seeking reps 81
    Faulty/troublesome 89
    Dishonest 91–93
    Matching to customers 112

Wanamaker, John 31
Web-based Directories 70, 180
Websites 24–26, 59, 127–130
Weiss, Alan (author) 21

11355103R0011

Made in the USA
Lexington, KY
27 September 2011